RESOURCE GUIDES FOR TEACHERS

Series editor: Michael Buckby

GERMAN/DEUTSCH

Peter Boaks

The views expressed in this publication are the author's and do not necessarily represent those of CILT.

Acknowledgements

The publishers wish to thank the following copyright holders for permission to reproduce copyright material:

cover	Poster mit Genehmigung des Goethe-Instituts, Zentralverwaltung.
p1	Fritz-Ullrich Fack, *Frankfurter Allgemeine Zeitung*, 2./3.10.1990.
p4	*Discovering German*, Goethe-Institut, London.
p19	*Jugendmagazin/Tip*, JUMA/TIP, Januar 1991.
p30	Pat Pattison, *Developing communications skills*, pp 33/34. Cambridge University Press, 1987.
p36	Mit Genehmigung entnommen aus *Deutsch Konkret*, Langenscheidt-Verlag Berlin und München.
p42	Mit Genehmigung entnommen aus *Deutsch Konkret*, Langenscheidt-Verlag Berlin und München.

It has not been possible in all cases to trace copyright-holders; the publishers would be glad to hear from any such unacknowledged copyright-holder.

First published 1991
© 1991 Centre for Information on Language Teaching and Research
ISBN 0 948003 49 9

Cover design by Logos Design & Advertising
Printed in Great Britain by Direct Printers Ltd

Published by Centre for Information on Language Teaching and Research, Regent's College, Inner Circle, Regents Park, London NW1 4NS.

All rights reserved. No part of the publication may be reproduced, stored in a retrieval system, or transmitted in any form or by any means, electronic, mechanical, photocopying, recording, or otherwise, without the prior permission of the Copyright owner.

Contents

		Page
Introduction		1
1	**German in the curriculum**	4
	Staffing - Timetabling German as FL1 and as FL2 - Primary Schools - Adult Education.	
2	**Certificates and examinations**	8
	Graded Objectives and Graded Assessment - GCSE - RSA - FLIC - Institute of Linguists - FLAW - IEE - City and Guilds - BTEC and CPVE - I-Level - Core Studies - Advanced Supplementary level - 'A' level - International Baccalaureate - ICC.	
3	**Using published teaching materials**	13
	What is available? - What do I need? - Accessibility - Listening materials - Motivation - Equal opportunities - Textbooks - Sources and resources: TV, video, radio, film - Magazines - Computer software.	
4	**Exploiting your own resources**	21
	Using realia and authentic materials - Exploiting the materials - Literature - Copyright - Using authentic audio, video, satellite TV - Equipment.	
5	**Teaching and learning styles**	27
	Changing needs - Differentiation - Teaching from the front - Group-work and pair-work - Errors - Grammar - Communicative activities - Independent learning - Organising the classroom - Drama and music - The technological and vocational approach - Special educational needs - Language awareness - Use of the foreign language and of English.	
6	**Bringing the country into the class**	35
	The German assistant - Class-to-class links - Electronic mail - Classroom displays - Dialects and songs - Slides, films, videos, posters.	
7	**School travel and exchange visits**	37
	Group tours - Home stays - Courses - Exchanges - Work experience - Tips on running school journeys - Planning an exchange.	
8	**Assessing progress**	41
	What is the purpose of assessment? - What do you assess? - How do you assess? - Marking - Self-assessment - Formative and summative assessment - Profiling -	

National Curriculum - Examination entries - Examination preparation - Scheme of work.

9   Taking it further 47
Languages and careers - Choosing the right course - Lingua - General or specialised skills? - The Languages Lead Body.

10   Professional development 49
Language skills - Methodology - School-based in-service training - Funding.

Useful addresses 51

In the text, * indicates that the address of the organisation mentioned is listed in this section.

Introduction

Das Alte stürzt, es ändert sich die Zeit,
Und neues Leben blüht aus den Ruinen.

In 1989 the walls dividing Europe came tumbling down. In the 1990s the European Community seeks to establish an even freer movement of capital, goods, workers and ideas and the peoples of Central and Eastern Europe, having seized their independence, can see at last the chance of a place in the sun within a whole, free and prosperous Europe.

In 1989 images of Germany crowded the media - dancing on the wall in Berlin, people-power in Leipzig, families united, hopes and fears for the future, the all-powerful Deutschmark, the re-emergence of an economic and cultural super-power straddling West and East like a colossus.

Germany, Germans and the German language are on everyone's agenda.

There are over 100 million native speakers of German and the Goethe-Institut estimates that there are a further sixteen million learners of German as a foreign language world-wide. A large proportion of these learners (over nine million) are citizens of the Soviet Union. Perhaps that should not surprise us in view of the traditional role which German occupied as lingua franca of Central Europe. The growing economic and political importance of the European Community and of Germany in particular has rendered obsolete Anglo-Saxon assumptions about the absence of any need to learn a foreign language. In addition, foreign languages make an important contribution to education in general and to cultural and European understanding.

Certainly H M Government has been proclaiming for some time the urgent need for more German teaching both of basic foreign language skills and of the advanced and specialised skills required by business and industry. Germany is our largest single trading partner and if we wish to turn deficit into surplus we must understand and cultivate that market from the inside - they will sell to us in English but we must sell to them in German.

How dramatically different is the context within which we now teach German compared with the situation of even a few years ago - German only for those able linguists who were already good at French; German for those who wished to escape from Latin - into German taught like Latin! Anyone who took or taught 'O' level will tell you that German is **difficult** - cases and double prepositions. Remember those pictures you had to describe in the 'oral' - Where is this man standing? Where is he going? Remember the 'comprehension' passages - *Die Tomaten sind unter den Kühlschrank gerollt - wo sind die Tomaten?*

The communicative revolution in foreign language teaching which began in the 1970s and swept the board in the 1980s has at last made German accessible to learners of all abilities, ages and aptitudes. After all, in the real world competence in a foreign language is demonstrably useful.

Popular TV courses and thriving adult evening classes, Graded Objectives and Graded Assessment schemes in schools, the new examinations - GCSE and Standard Grade, 'AS', new 'A' level courses and a whole range of other practical and vocational qualifications now on offer - all these developments testify to the relevance of German as a main objective or, perhaps more significantly, as an important enhancement of other specialisms - Accountancy and German, Business Studies and German, Engineering and German, etc.

However, the most important principle of the communicative approach (and of the *Kontaktschwelle* - Threshold Level - defined by the Council of Europe) is precisely this **communication** between cultures and between individuals of all ages, the widening of horizons and the fostering of a spirit of enquiry and understanding through enjoyment and contact - in short the bringing down of real or imagined walls.

WOZU?

This book aims to encourage and support the teaching of German in schools, colleges and centres of Adult Education by offering general principles, practical tips and a guide to sources of information, teaching materials and methods, curriculum organisation and examinations.

It aims to help individual teachers of German make well-informed decisions about ways to promote both their subject and their own professional development.

FÜR WEN?

★ Those teaching (or training to teach) German in the United Kingdom.

★ Those currently teaching another language and contemplating offering German also.

★ Teachers, Heads of Department, Headteachers, Governors or Modern Languages Advisers considering introducing German in their schools or colleges.

WARUM GERADE JETZT?

The inclusion of a foreign language in the National Curriculum as a Foundation Subject entitlement for all 11-16-year-olds, with programmes of study, attainment targets and statements of attainment, has given foreign language teaching a new high profile. Alongside the two statutory requirements of extension and assessment, the DES is anxious to promote a policy of diversification of the first foreign language offered in schools. Of all the languages other than French currently taught, it is German which is best placed to provide that alternative.

GCSE entries for 1989 show a total of 265, 239 for French and 77,067 for German. At 'A' level the totals were 21,890 for French and 7,705 for German. This puts German clearly in second place, some way ahead of its nearest rival, Spanish.

A broadly similar situation exists in Scotland. In Northern Ireland, German is to be found mainly as a second foreign language for able linguists within a largely selective school system.

Different ways in which German can be offered will be discussed in the next chapter.

At all levels there has been an enormous increase in the amount and range of commercially produced teaching material now available. This, coupled with the quite exceptional support offered by the Goethe-Institut and other organisations in Germany, means that no teacher of German need worry about the availability of teaching resources and specialist advice. The problem is knowing what is available, where to obtain it and how to use it.

WAS? WO? WIE?

The chapters which follow will offer some answers to these and other questions.

Find out more by reading:

DES *General Certificate of Secondary Education, the National Criteria: French.* HMSO (1985)

Hagen, S (ed) *Languages in British business: an analysis of current needs.* Newcastle Polytechnic/CILT (1988)

King, A, G Thomas, D Hewett *Languages and careers: an information pack.* CILT (1989)

Phillips, D (ed) *Languages in schools: from complacency to conviction.* CILT (1988)

Littlewood, W *Communicative language teaching - an introduction.* CUP (1981)

DES, Report of the National Curriculum Modern Foreign Languages Working Group: *Modern Foreign Languages for ages 11 to 16.* HMSO (1990)

1 German in the curriculum

Der Mann, der das Wenn und das Aber erdacht,
Hätt' sicher aus Häckerling Gold schon gemacht.

However convincing the reasons for teaching German may be, we still have to fit it into a crowded school and national curriculum. With a substantial and prescribed National Curriculum of Core and Foundation subjects - including one foreign language for all in the Key Stages 3 and 4 / S3/S4 (11-16) - it is vital for the success of **diversification** that we find ways to offer German as that first foreign language (FL1). The traditional role of German as second foreign language (FL2) will also need to be considered.

How can we offer German?

STAFFING

There is a shortage of all language teachers,

but

- German is second only to French in numbers of learners and teachers.

- Many French specialists have subsidiary German.

- There may be 'inactive' German teachers who could be persuaded and helped to return to the profession.

- Schools or LEAs might recruit untrained 'licensed teachers' - perhaps native speakers.

- Teachers might be recruited from other EC countries.

Ask your Local Education Authority Adviser or Inspector for Languages about their policy for diversification and for training or re-training 'non-specialists' who could teach German.

Make the case to your governing body with the aid of the *'Discovering German'* brochure produced by the Goethe-Institut* (1990).

TIMETABLING

German as sole FL1

This depends on actual and projected availability of specialist staff and on persuading Headteachers, Governors and parents that it is a good idea. The vocational and economic prospects and the broader cultural and educational perspective discussed in the Introduction will help you to make your case.

German as alternate or equal FL1

This can make a school more attractive to its potential customers. Headteachers and Governors can easily be persuaded of the advantages for the school's image. The problems arise when you look at the details. Nevertheless, this is the most likely route to diversification since it offers flexibility when faced with staffing constraints.

In fact, for a school of at least four forms of entry the 'split' offer of equal FL1 is the preferred DES model.

These are some of the points you will have to consider:

Alternate, e.g. this year's beginners all do French, next year's all do German.

Pro
- Simple.
- Time to think, prepare and coordinate all staff, year by year.
- Practical for a small school.

Contra
- Do you have equal staffing strength in French and German?
- Will timetabling constraints mean that you have classes taught by 'non-specialists?'
- 'Transfers-in' - pupils transferred from another school where FL1 was French may find themselves in a wholly German year group.

Split, e.g. half of entry does German, half does French (or 60/40 or whatever).

Pro
- Usually allows greater staffing flexibility as probably fewer teachers of the same language will be required simultaneously.
- Both languages are perceived as equal in every year.
- Continuity.

Contra
- Do you allow choice - free, guided or dictated with exceptions made for those who object?
- Does the language split determine House or Form?
- Can be unpopular with school management.

Mixed, e.g. this year's beginners do French **or** German, next year's do French **or** Spanish (**or** German).

Pro
- Flexible if staffing is uncertain. You can vary your total commitment each year by adjusting Year 1.
- You can run three or more languages.

Contra
- If you split too many ways you may find that one of the languages offered has too few learners to permit:
  a) setting - if you wish to set;
  b) viable 'A' level group sizes. On the other hand, there has been increased take-up at 'A' level since the introduction of GCSE.

Carousel - Various schemes exist for 'taster' courses in perhaps three languages over one or two years followed by a free choice of one as first foreign language. It is likely that the need to reach targets in Key Stage 3 of the National Curriculum will rule out this approach.

German as FL2

The view of HMI as expressed in *Curriculum Matters 8* (1987) and *Modern Languages in the School Curriculum* (1988) was that FL2 offered in 'lower school' (i.e. 11-14) had often not produced sufficient 'takers' at 14 plus and on these grounds could not be considered a success. Where additional time had been given to FL2 this had unbalanced the whole curriculum to the detriment of other useful subjects. It has been DES policy to encourage *ab initio* courses in FL2 in Key Stage 4 'for able and committed linguists'.

Needless to say, this view caused much controversy. The Staff Inspector in office at the time has since acknowledged that this was a mistake and that FL2 should begin earlier. The National Curriculum Working Group was keen to support FL2, but it remains true that the arrival of National Curriculum targets in all Core and Foundation subjects has further increased the pressure on 'extra' subjects in Key Stage 3.

FL1 is, of course, a foundation subject and it will not be practical to use some of its minimum 'reasonable amount of time' - probably 10% - for FL2. FL2 is not part of the National Curriculum but, in practice, pupils will consider it more seriously as an option if there is proper certification: GCSE, Graded Objectives, etc. The National Curriculum proposals would allow a pupil to choose FL2 as the 'foundation' language at Key Stage 4 in any case.

In fact, despite the pressures on FL2 in the 11-16 curriculum, there are a number of good arguments and some practical strategies in its favour.

- Research (see David Phillips' book: *Which language?* Hodder and Stoughton, 1989) has shown that the 'customers' regard the offer of more than one foreign language as important and attractive - even if, when faced with difficult choices, relatively few pupils continue with two languages.

- School management will be keen to enhance the image and status of the school when competing for intake.

- Graded Assessment/Graded Objectives make it possible to plan a coherent short-term course with a certificate at the end of it.

Who should be offered the chance to learn FL2?

All learners 11-16?

Pro
- Democratic.
- Gives you a better chance of recruiting a viable option group for FL2 in Key Stage 4.

Contra
- Expensive. Twice the number of textbooks, etc.
- Some customer resistance if compulsory.

Selected able classes or pupils?

Pro
- May be more realistic in terms of staffing and resources.
- Rapid progress possible with a class of able learners.

Contra
- On what basis and when do you choose?
- Divisive, élitist.
- What do the rest do instead?

How do we fit it in?

Start in Year 1 - equal amount of time for each language.

Pro
- High profile for languages.
- Another certificate or qualification.

Contra
- Unless languages receive a larger share of the timetable you will have insufficient time to reach targets in whichever language is the Foundation subject.

Start in Year 2 or 3, e.g. take some time from FL1 and plan a self-contained shorter course leading to a Graded Objectives Certificate by the end of Key Stage 3.

Pro
- Allows time for pupils to experience and consolidate FL1 before teaching FL2.

Contra
- Too little time for FL2 reduces its status in the eyes of the learner. Only one lesson per week, for example, is too tenuous a thread for many pupils.

As an option in Key Stage 4

Pro
- Simple, self-selecting.
- Economical.
- Does not affect time available for FL1.

Contra
- Cramming for GCSE - is it desirable?
- Only for academically able pupils?
- Smaller option groups may not be viable.

As an extra-curricular activity in 'dawn' or in 'twilight time'

Teachers of community languages such as Turkish and Urdu have often had to devise ingenious ways of offering them. Make further enquiries via your LEA. The National Curriculum Working Group recommends a flexible approach to timetabling in order to accommodate FL2. Some schools offer community access to such classes - definitely a plus in terms of public relations.

Ab initio post-16

With the prospect of core skills in 16-19 there will be opportunities for 'new' languages post-16. This provides another opportunity for German.

GERMAN IN PRIMARY SCHOOLS

The government has funded twelve pilot schemes for the teaching of a modern European foreign language in primary schools (French, German, Spanish and Italian) in Scotland. In addition, several local authorities have begun parallel piloting.

In Strathclyde, for example, the specialist language teaching input will be made by the modern languages department of the local secondary school, but primary teachers will receive training in order to ensure that the language teaching is fully integrated into the primary curriculum. This means that in Strathclyde alone some seventeen primary schools will have experience of offering German. Meanwhile, other LEAs in the UK are experimenting with primary foreign languages, including German.

Send for the CILT* information sheets on: *Teaching languages to young beginners: reports and guides* and *German for young beginners: teaching materials*.

GERMAN IN ADULT EDUCATION

Secondary school teachers of German can at last see a higher status for all languages and, despite the type of practical problems listed above, a promising future for German.

In the adult and further education sector the picture has long been positive. Here learners are free agents and self-motivating to a degree rare in the compulsory 11-16 sector. Some colleges have developed innovative modular courses and individual learning programmes. The point for teachers in the secondary sector is that much of what is successful in the FE and Adult Education world today may well be feasible for schools tomorrow.

Send for the CILT* information sheets on: *Language courses for adults (part-time and intensive)* and *Teaching materials for adults: German*.

Teachers in Adult Education often work in comparative isolation. Stay in touch with developments by joining *NETWORD* - the national network supporting languages tutors in Adult Education. Write to CILT* for further details.

Find out more by reading:

DES *Modern languages in the school curriculum: a statement of policy.* HMSO (1988)

DES *Modern foreign languages to 16.* HMI Series: Curriculum Matters 8. HMSO (1987)

Phillips, D *Which language? Diversification and the National Curriculum.* Hodder and Stoughton (1989)

Calvert, M *Towards diversification.* LMDU University of York (1989)

DES *An inquiry into practice in 22 comprehensive schools where a foreign language forms part of the curriculum for all or almost all pupils up to age 16.* HMSO (1987)

CILT* information sheet *The National Curriculum and modern foreign languages: basic list of documents.*

NFER* *Diversification of Foreign Languages in Schools* - Report on the ESG Pilot Programme (1990)

2 Certificates and examinations

Es führen viele Wege nach Rom.

Graded Objectives and Graded Assessment - the road to languages for all

The success of short-term courses with practical 'can do' objectives and tests which reward positive achievement, however limited, has been a major factor in making foreign languages accessible to all learners over the last decade. German, once considered 'difficult' because of its case system and word order, has benefited enormously from this change of attitude. Across the country, groups of teachers produced defined syllabuses based on real-life language use in everyday situations with tests of competence which rewarded getting the message (i.e. understanding the essentials) and getting your message across (i.e. speaking well enough to be understood even if you make mistakes).

Syllabuses were clearly defined and included, for example, topic headings giving specific **functions**, e.g. ask the way to a place; general **notions** usable in various contexts, e.g. telling the time; and often vocabulary lists of useful words for recognition or use. The point is that the learner should understand the objectives and be able to achieve them step by step. This type of syllabus is not a teaching programme or scheme of work but a framework or checklist of **minimum** not **maximum** targets.

GOML (Graded Objectives in Modern Languages) schemes of this type usually have a syllabus for each level. Sometimes there is a test after each unit within a level, nearly always there is a test in Listening, Reading, Speaking (plus Writing at the higher levels). Each level is usually completed in one or, at most, two years. Pupil/student self-assessment is built into some schemes and can be an important motivator. A certificate is awarded for success at each level.

If your local authority does not operate a Graded Objectives scheme it is possible to use one from another authority. The library at CILT* has a record of all GOML schemes. Find out more by reading: *Languages step by step: graded objectives in the UK*, Page, B and D Hewett (CILT, 1987) and *GOML News* from CILT.

The status of a Graded Test certificate varies from totally informal to officially recognised - for example the NEA* (Northern Examining Association) will **endorse** Levels 1-3 of any approved scheme with its own statement to be added to the certificate. The GAML (Graded Assessment in Modern Languages) scheme of LEAG* (London and East Anglian Group) offers GCSE accreditation at every level from beginners to 16+ and is based on a monitored programme of **continuous** assessment. The French scheme was granted full GCSE status in 1989 with the German scheme to follow soon after. This may represent the next generation of the graded assessment revolution. Send to LEAG* for further information. Ask other examination boards for information on any similar schemes.

GCSE

If you are not acquainted with the style and requirements of the existing GCSE examinations you should obtain copies of the syllabus and past papers. Chief Examiners' reports and information for teachers on assessing skills and conducting the oral examinations are also very useful.

In Scotland contact the Scottish Examination Board* to find out about Standard Grade.

In the rest of the UK contact:
The Midlands Examining Group (MEG)*
The Northern Examining Association (NEA)*
The Southern Examining Group (SEG)*
   (Ask about their modular or course-work GCSE also)
The London and East Anglian Group (LEAG)*
   (Ask about GAML also - see above)
The Northern Ireland Schools Examining Council (NISEC)*
The Welsh Joint Education Committee*

Send to CILT* for information sheet: *GCSE examining groups: language examinations on offer.*

The main characteristics of the GCSE and Standard Grade are:

★ realistic tasks in realistic situations from the most basic level to the highest level;
★ credit given for communicating, especially at basic level, with accuracy and wider command of language rewarded at the higher levels.

These characteristics are reflected also in other examinations available to learners of German post-16:

Royal Society of Arts

The RSA examinations are intended for full-time or part-time students in Further or Adult Education. They could also be used post-16 in schools. There are four levels ranging from a standard approximating to a Basic Level GCSE up to a level of competence sufficiently advanced to enable the candidate to undertake a Higher Education course.

The syllabus and examinations are 'communicative' in nature. *German Levels 1-4 modern languages examinations, explanatory booklet and syllabus guidelines* is in itself an interesting document if you are teaching to any communicative syllabus.

The RSA offers also more vocational and specialised qualifications suitable for adults. For this and further information on their commercial and business certificates contact the Royal Society of Arts Examination Board*.

Foreign Languages for Industry and Commerce (FLIC)

These examinations assess the candidate's communicative effectiveness in 'sympathetic, work-orientated exchanges'. The examinations test speaking and listening skills and can be taken at any time (one month's notice required). The test is conducted by trained external examiners.

There are four levels.

For further information contact the London Chamber of Commerce and Industry*.

Institute of Linguists

This is one of the foremost language examining bodies in Britain with a wide range of specialist courses for specific professions. It also offers examinations for the general public via adult education or further education colleges.

These are realistic task-based examinations designed for those who need to use German in their job or career.

There are five levels ranging from beginners to second class degree level.

For further information contact the Institute of Linguists*. Ask for the brochure on Examinations in languages for international communication, the Administrative handbook and specimen material.

Foreign Languages at Work (FLAW)

This scheme is run jointly by the London Chamber of Commerce, the British Overseas Trade Board and the University of Oxford Delegacy of Local Examinations. It is designed to cater for those students (post-16) who would benefit from continuing foreign language studies alongside their other specialisms. The course is designed to follow on from GCSE or can be an *ab initio* course in a new foreign language.

Students apply their linguistic knowledge and develop practical skills by 'putting the foreign languages to work' in transactions and general tasks related to the world of work and business and social contacts with Germany.

An important characteristic of FLAW is that **teachers design and submit for approval their own course** which should stress practical and oral use of German and a wide range of authentic materials. Each student is assessed continuously throughout the course. A dossier of assignments, including a cassette of recordings made by the student and evidence of student self-assessment, is examined by the teacher and by an external moderator.

This scheme is very flexible and is working successfully with sixth forms and Further and Adult Education Institutions. It is a useful alternative to 'A' or 'AS' courses for many students.

Send for the booklet *Foreign languages at work scheme* from the London Chamber of Commerce Examination Board*.

IEE Preliminary Certificate of Modern Language Skills for Work

The Institute of European Education* at Lancaster has developed a modular scheme leading to the award of a certificate by the IEE itself or, if you prefer, flexible enough to fit in to any other **pre-vocational** course.

It aims to prepare students to deal with foreign visitors to Britain in a range of work situations in the tourist/service industries.

There is an emphasis on self-assessment and also personal and social skills. A 210-page 'twinfile' pack containing notes, checklists, profiling statement, banks, etc can be purchased from the Institute of European Education*. There is also a pack of accompanying teaching materials.

City and Guilds

Modular options in German are available. They are based on course-work assignments with GCSE-style assessment criteria.

Further information from: The City and Guilds of London Institute*.

BTEC (Business and Technician Education Council) and CPVE (Certificate of Pre-vocational Education)

These vocational and pre-vocational courses cover a wide range of subjects in an integrated and modular approach. Students work on practical projects with the assistance of the teacher and learn through doing the project, with teaching geared to the completion of tasks and assignments.

If your institution offers these, your best plan is to consult the co-ordinator or whoever oversees the whole programme in your school or college since you will need to understand the philosophy behind them.

BTEC* offers Foreign Language Units aimed at developing skills in using a language in the workplace. The emphasis is on assignments and problem-solving. BTEC National is in effect an alternative to 'A' or 'AS' level. A handbook giving guidelines and unit specifications can be purchased from:

Publications Despatch Unit, BTEC*.

CPVE has no modules in language work but German can be included under the teaching of Travel and Tourism. In some cases students add on a course such as the IEE* (see above) to their main CPVE programme.

York I-Level

The University of York Certificate of Achievement at an Intermediate/Supplementary level is aimed at those students wishing to continue a practical and general course post-16 but who wish to specialise in other subject areas. It is offered in German and French.

Reasonable proficiency is essential but the syllabus has limited objectives - for example, coping with problems, using the telephone, participation in discussion, extensive and intensive reading, etc.

Further details, teaching and testing materials are available from:

The Publications Office, University of York Language Materials Development Unit*.

Core Studies 16-19

In 1989 the Government called for a common core of skills for all post-16 courses. These skills would include communications, information technology, numeracy and a foreign language.

The Associated Examining Board* has a range of modular syllabuses which can be used as part of an 'A' level, 'AS' level, BTEC* or RSA* course. Pilot schemes have had some success and this may well represent a major opportunity for German as part of a broader general education in the 16-19 sector. Ask for information on the Wessex Project.

'AS' - Advanced Supplementary level

These courses were introduced in the late 1980s in order to broaden the traditional pattern of 'A' level studies in schools and colleges. Higher Education identified modern languages as a priority area for 'AS'. They offer a qualification of 'A' level standard but are based on a more restricted syllabus enabling them to be studied in half the teaching and studying time. In practice, this usually means a two-year course in parallel with other 'A' levels and sometimes with another 'AS'.

As a high level, extra qualification for specialists in other subject areas such as Science, they represent a considerable opportunity for foreign languages. The 'AS' syllabuses promote, in effect, new-style communicative language courses **minus** the background topic/literature element contained in 'A' level. They follow on well from GCSE courses and it is usually possible to combine 'A' and 'AS' students in the same language class - especially if the 'A' level students are following a new-style syllabus (see below) which has a similar approach to reading and listening comprehension and use of language.

Syllabuses and specimen materials for 'AS' are available from the 'A' level examination boards (see below) and are well worth acquiring and studying in detail since they have many implications for teaching materials and methods.

Write to CILT* for information sheet *Guide to GCE 'AS' level examinations*.

'A' - Advanced level GCE

Traditionally almost the only target offered post-16 and still for most the key to language study in Higher Education.

The entry requirements for degree courses at universities have held enormous sway over examinations and courses in secondary schools. Usually this meant an emphasis on prose translation and discussion (in English) of literary works. Old-style 'A' level German (still available) was precisely tailored for the requirements of the traditional 'literary' degree in German.

Now Higher Education has diversified and also offers courses with a current affairs/media/business emphasis, so the whole question of what constitutes '... *a sound base of the skills, language and attitudes required for further study...*' (GCSE National Criteria) has had to be re-assessed. Indeed, the mismatch between GCSE and 'A' level syllabuses - although often exaggerated - highlights further the problem of continuity of objectives and approaches.

The result has been alternative, new-style 'A' level syllabuses which are communicative and practical rather than academic and abstract. The emphasis is on greater use of the foreign language, on authentic non-literary texts and 'relevant' themes with literature in context. This does not necessarily mean the end of the classical approach and literary appreciation, but it does offer you and your students a choice.

CILT* has compiled an information leaflet (No. 10) *Guide to GCE 'A' level examinations.*

The University of Oxford Delegacy* and the JMB* offer perhaps the most radical approach with ULSEB* and the AEB* taking more of a middle course. JMB* also offers a coursework option.

It is vital that you obtain as much material and information as possible about each syllabus before making a decision.

As with 'AS', there are considerable implications for materials and methods. Fortunately, the Goethe-Institut* offers a wealth of suitable material (see Chapter 3) and the CILT* publication *German for 'A' level - a resource-based approach* has practical advice on methods.

International Baccalaureate

This internationally recognised qualification has considerable potential for future development in the new Europe. It offers a broader approach than 'A' level, with six subjects at two levels, and has been successfully introduced into some schools in the UK.

For more information contact International Baccalaureate*. See also the House of Lords report, May, 1990.

International Certificate Conference (ICC)

This is an international association of adult education organisations which have adopted the language certificate programme devised by the Deutscher Volkshochschulverband* (DVV).

SUMMARY

There is a syllabus in German to suit you and your students.

The wide variety of syllabus content and assessment styles simply mirrors the range of real-life language demands and emphasises the importance of foreign languages.

Ensure that the students (and their parents) understand the aims and the requirements of the course. From the most basic graded test through to 'A' level they need to know both the destination and the purpose of their journey.

Using published teaching materials 3

Die Spreu vom Weizen sondern.

The aim of this chapter is to help you identify what you need, to describe in general terms what is available and to suggest criteria for selecting teaching materials.

Does one follow a textbook or is it better to put together one's own package from various sources?

In recent years the trend, honoured perhaps more in advice and intention than in practice, has been away from 'all-in' course books and towards a new 'resource-based' approach. Usually teachers go for a mixed economy, somewhere on a continuum between the two extremes of total submission to a published course and total reliance on home-assembled 'original' or plagiarised materials. Whichever way you lean, you will need to filter, adapt and organise your resources to suit your own situation and students.

WHAT IS AVAILABLE?

Fortunately there is now available a large range of published material for German.

★ Complete courses - books, tapes, OHTs, etc.
★ Books, tapes designed to develop particular skills, e.g. listening, role-plays, etc.
★ TV/video/radio programmes with accompanying books or notes.
★ Filmstrips, slides.
★ Magazines designed for learners.
★ Computer software.

Teachers of German are particularly fortunate in having easy access to the published resources of the Goethe-Institut* and to numerous publications from Germany - many of them **free** (details below).

WHAT DO I NEED?

Look for materials which:

- relate to the content of the examination syllabus or the areas of experience of National Curriculum programmes of study, i.e. cover most of the topic areas. The sequence of topics is not that important. Within any one key stage your graded objectives or graded assessment syllabus is a checklist or framework for your programme of work. It cannot and should not dictate everything you do. Usually these syllabuses are flexible enough for you to choose the order of modules or topics anyway.

- can be used as part of a **structured** or progressive course, i.e. a course in which you **build up** the ability to use the language and understand the way it works. Modern 'complete' courses aim to build up a framework of grammar and structures by using these in a particular real-life situation, e.g. modal verbs and school life - what you must, may, can or cannot do! Structures and topics are recycled and developed over the whole course.

- are **appropriate** to the age-group. Mimicking adult transactions should not predominate in a lower school course. Look for materials and activities which encourage learners to use their German in a variety of contexts. Real life is unpredictable and both children and adults need to be able to manipulate the language enough to get their own message across.

- provide intellectual **challenge,** integrate cultural information and issues and encourage a creative and imaginative use of language.

It is most important to look for materials which give you and your students an opportunity to develop and practise the **skills** and **competences** described in your syllabus and in your scheme of work (see Chapter 8).

Look for this:

Although defined separately here, these skills are of course often mixed in real life and your materials need to reflect this in the tasks set. The Attainment Targets of the National Curriculum enshrine this principle.

LISTENING
★ authentic, natural speed, regional accents;
★ unscripted, well scripted;
★ short and extended texts;
★ announcements, advertisements, monologues, dialogues, discussions, accounts, songs, stories, jokes;
★ factual, transactional, interactional, persuasive, discursive, imaginative language;
★ range of language registers - formal, informal.

READING
★ authentic or well devised, printed, handwritten;
★ short and extended texts;
★ signs, notices, announcements, advertisements, notes, messages, letters, reports, articles, stories, poems, cartoons, comic strips;
★ factual, transactional, interactional, persuasive, discursive, imaginative language;
★ range of language registers - formal, informal.

Skills
- Understand:
  gist, selected details, most or all details.

- Identify:
  ideas, attitudes, feelings.

- See:
  relationships between different parts of a text.

- Draw:
  inferences and conclusions.

SPEAKING
★ stimulus: pictures, visual cues, listening cues, printed word cues, instructions for role-plays, general conversation and discussion;
★ predictable and unpredictable situations/role-plays, information and opinion-gap activities, open-ended situations and discussions;
★ transactional and interactional practice;
★ formal and informal register.

WRITING
★ stimulus: pictures, visual cues, notes, postcards, instructions, messages, letters, articles;
★ write notes, postcards, messages, instructions, letters, reports, articles, accounts, stories, poems, songs, jokes;
★ transactional and interactional writing;
★ formal and informal register.

Some important language activities to look out for:

- Ask and answer questions.
- Get your message across.
- Adapt and transfer between contexts/situations.
- Informed use of communication strategies which help to cope with new language and new situations (see NEA* GCSE French syllabus).
- Cope with the unexpected. React and make suggestions.
- Give an opinion and persuade others. Discuss.
- Express feelings.
- Narrate events.
- Create (e.g. a story, a poem, a TV commercial, a tourist brochure).

Many of these skills should be part of the learning objectives from the very beginning of your course. They cannot be acquired suddenly, at a late stage. Where appropriate, they should be mixed, not separated. Do the published materials you are considering help you to develop these skills?

ARE THE MATERIALS ACCESSIBLE TO ALL OR MOST LEARNERS?

The **materials** you use can be either a bridge or a barrier between you and the student and between the student and the language.

```
                                                        WORTE
                                                        WORTE
                                                        WORTE
                                                        WORTE
                                                        WORTE
            WORTE WORTE WORTE                           WORTE
         WORTE WORTE WORTE WORTE                        WORTE
       WORTE                  WORTE                     WORTE
       WORTE                  WORTE                     WORTE
       WORTE                  WORTE                     WORTE
       WORTE                  WORTE                     WORTE
                                                        WORTE
    ICH                            DU                   WORTE
                                                        WORTE
                                                        WORTE
                                                   DU   WORTE   ICH
```

(Renate Welsh)

Lesespaß (Langenscheidt, 1989)

For example, pages of closely packed text with few 'signposts' or graphical devices to point out what is important, uniform small print or unattractive design are major barriers to the majority of students.

Nowadays, everyone in the western world is visually literate to a degree inconceivable even in the recent past. Everything in our lives is designed to attract attention, please the eye and communicate a message effectively. Contrast, for example, the style and impact of children's Saturday morning television with the presentation in the average school textbook. Why should young people take the latter seriously? Teachers usually like solidly organised books with lots of **work**! Students have a different perspective.

The following characteristics make printed material more **accessible** to **all** learners and thus more **effective**:

★ it addresses the **student** not the **teacher**;

★ page layout is open and varied - not uniform and dull;

★ meaning or main points are highlighted by headlines, captions, illustrations, shading, colouring or other devices;

★ pictures/illustrations are relevant, interesting, amusing;

★ instructions, rubrics, etc are short and clear - whether in English or in German;

★ tasks are varied and have a clear point, both to teacher and student;

★ some tasks are open-ended and give the students a choice or the opportunity to be creative.

The last two points are vital and too often ignored.

A book which consists largely of many repetitive and very guided exercises and drills prepares students for only a very limited range of FL use and thus easily stifles the initiative and enthusiasm of teacher and learner - yet both these qualities are crucial to success in foreign language learning.

The ways in which learners acquire a new language are complex and individual. You need to distinguish between two types of activity: one type concentrates on the medium or process of communication, i.e. it is **pre-communicative**. Practice drills, grammar exercises, games with words would come into this category.

The other type is **communicative**, where the message, received or conveyed, is the focus. A task in a textbook should be set in a real context:

- **not**: *'What is on every floor of this department store?'*
  but rather: *'What presents would you want to buy and where might you find them?'*

- **not**: *'Describe the people in this picture'*
  but rather: *'Describe someone you know to your partner and see if he/she can guess who it is.'*

At all levels, teacher and materials together should help learners to:

1. cope with understanding a new listening or reading text;
2. check that essentials have been understood;
3. practise use of language in carefully guided exercises;
4. move on to less guided tasks with opportunities to improvise;
5. use what has been learnt in an open-ended and creative way. At the simplest level this could mean writing one word in a speech bubble in a cartoon, at an intermediate level it could mean making genuinely original or personal contributions to a conversation and at a higher level a contribution to a discussion or a piece of creative and original writing.

The art of matching the exercise to the objective in this way is expounded in a very thorough and practical way in *Übungstypologie zum kommunikativen Deutschunterricht* (Neuner, G, M Krüger, U Grewer, Langenscheidt, 1981).

LISTENING MATERIAL - WHAT TYPES ARE SUITABLE?

As with printed material it is important to be clear about the type and purpose of taped listening material.

For example, dialogues which are intended as a model for the students' own production may be quite different in style from conversations where the student has to 'listen in' in order to catch the gist of what is being said. You need both types.

Listening input is of course crucial, whether it comes live from teacher or assistant or recorded from audio tape or video. Try to **hear** before you **buy**. You could use the following criteria as a checklist:

★ Is the voice right or convincing, e.g. not an adult pretending to be a young person?
★ Is there a variety of different voices?
★ Acoustic, background sounds. Are they appropriate without being obtrusive?
★ Speed, delivery. Are they natural or forced?
★ Language register and vocabulary. Are they natural and authentic?

The way in which the material has been produced is also significant:

★ Is there any 'off-air' broadcast material?
★ Are there any real unscripted interviews done on location?
★ Where a script or scenario is used in a studio recording, is the production such that the result sounds convincing? Is it realistic and authentic?

A scenario is an outline of what the speakers have to say. They then phrase it and interact as they see fit. The scenario method is normally used for producing GCSE listening tests and some teaching materials for listening also. However, in practice the results are often unsatisfactory, especially if amateurs are used. Hesitation, muttering, interruption, gabbled and garbled speech may be 'natural', but there are some hysterical examples published which are more difficult to understand than the real thing. Remember also that a disembodied voice from a loudspeaker, headphone (or telephone) is in any case denuded of all para-linguistic gestures and aids to comprehension.

A good script with professional actors and proper professional production can conjure up a complete sound-picture and thereby compensate for the inherent unnaturalness of the listener's situation. Recordings made in Germany will not use the same sterling *émigré* voices which we have come to know so well and should feature adult and teenage actors who are in daily touch with the style and sound of contemporary German.

Authentic unscripted interviews with schoolchildren or members of the public can come across with a directness which makes them surprisingly accessible - after all, the students do not have to understand every word. The same is true of real broadcast material.

WILL THE MATERIALS INTEREST AND MOTIVATE MY STUDENTS?

Obviously those factors which make material more **accessible** to students (see above) will help to motivate. Other important factors are **relevance** to their own lives, points of **contact** with their own experience and **contrasts** with their own culture.

Cultural differences which seem minor to us can be of considerable interest to young people. Books which include authentic material produced **for** or **by** the equivalent audience or age-group in Germany are inherently attractive and direct. The impact is lost, however, if they are exploited to death!

Material produced in Germany which has an authentic 'feel' will carry cultural messages in a natural way and may well stimulate a spirit of enquiry. Value for money does not necessarily come from a densely-packed book with lots of exercises and contrived text - especially if it turns many students off. Something which is visually attractive and different and offers things that you cannot easily provide yourself may prove a better investment.

EQUAL OPPORTUNITIES

Alles in der Welt läßt sich ertragen,
Nur nicht eine Reihe von schönen Tagen.

The stilted images of typical life and attitudes portrayed in foreign language teaching materials have traditionally been a source of great amusement. It is, however, surprising that so much published material still perpetuates social stereotypes which are at best over-simplified and unrealistic and at worst disheartening for students. Who would guess, judging by what is commonly used in schools, that not everyone has mum, dad, nice house, garden, dog and improving hobbies? Social, cultural, ethnic or even personal tensions rarely surface and everyone is so infuriatingly positive!

If it is important for your students to relate to the teaching materials, they should at least occasionally meet people whose hobby is hanging around rather than collecting stamps, whose sisters prefer metalwork to sewing and who heartily dislike school and sometimes even argue with their elders and betters!

TEXTBOOKS FOR 'A' AND 'AS'

A new generation of advanced level language courses with the emphasis on communicative activities and authentic texts is now appearing as the examination syllabuses change.

The examination boards themselves sometimes produce supporting materials - for example the University of Oxford Delegacy* has produced topic-based resource packs for its own syllabus.

See also: *German for 'A' level: a resource based approach* (CILT, 1985) and CILT information sheet *'A' level teaching materials: German*.

TEXTBOOKS FOR PRIMARY GERMAN

One course designed especially for early beginners is *Wer? Wie? Was?* (Nelson). Others are published in Germany (e.g. *Das Deutschmobil*) and are obtainable from the European Bookshop*.

The Muzzy Pack (BBC) is a complete multi-media course for children up to the age of twelve and available in French, German, Spanish and Italian. For further information write to Sales Office, BBC English*.

Send for the CILT information sheet: *German for young beginners - teaching materials*.

SOURCES AND RESOURCES: TV, VIDEO, RADIO, FILM

The BBC and Independent Television have produced a variety of teaching materials for German, usually supported by pupils' books, teachers' notes and cassettes. Try to integrate this material as part of your normal scheme of work rather than simply using it on a Friday afternoon when all else fails.

Some notable examples have been:

BBC

Deutsch Direkt (Adults), *Working in German/Talking of work: German* (TVEI, BTEC RSA), *Deutscher Club* ('A' level), *Deutsch für die Oberstufe. Lernexpress* (1990) (beginners to GCSE) consists of TV programmes with coursebook and audio cassettes. It can be used as the basis of a two-year *ab initio* GCSE course.

Full details of current broadcasts from: BBC Education*.

Educational institutions usually receive details of forthcoming broadcasts from the BBC and an emergency service for anyone who failed to record a particular broadcast is offered by the BBC School Radio Cassette Service, Broadcasting House, London W1A 1AA. The Language Centre, Brighton Polytechnic* runs courses in conjunction with the BBC on using broadcasts for teaching languages.

ITV (Thames TV)

Partner was an interesting series with supporting textbook, aimed at younger learners. *Videothek* is for GCSE.

Themes - Olympus Satellite/University of Oxford Language Teaching Centre

A series of one-hour packages for advanced learners. The TV component, consisting of extracts from TV news bulletins, is broadcast on the Olympus satellite.
Send to CILT for the information sheet on *Satellite TV and Olympus*.

Goethe-Institut

The Goethe-Institut*, with centres in London, Manchester, York and Glasgow, offers a range of materials: video cassettes; audio cassettes; slides; notes; dossiers and books which can be borrowed or bought. Ask for a catalogue. Some interesting examples are:

★ Video
- *Montags erste Stunde Deutsch* (13-15)
- *Klassenfest* (13-16)
- *German spoken here* and *Why learn German?* (beginners/option time)
- *Schule stellt sich vor* (13-16)
- numerous films or productions of literary works

★ Audio
- *Authentische Übungen zum Lese- und Hörverstehen für die GCSE - Prüfung*
- *Schülerporträts* (GCSE)
- *Porträts von deutschen Jugendlichen* (Advanced)

★ Computer
Software (Apple) is available: games, language exercises, gap-filling, etc (published by Langenscheidt).

★ Books
- *Schule und Freizeit* (GCSE)
- *Werbung und Anzeigen* (GCSE/Advanced)
- *Ausländische Jugendliche* (Advanced)

Each of these is accompanied by a volume of exercises and notes.

★ Dossiers
- On 'A' level topics

German Film and Video Library

A wide range of films and videos of particular interest to teachers of 'A' level groups. Ask for the catalogue and newsletters from VISCOM Limited*.

Inter Nationes

This is a valuable source of audio-visual material, mostly free (except video cassettes). Much of the material is for advanced learners but some is very suitable for GCSE and for beginners, especially as *Landeskunde*. Ask for the catalogue from Inter Nationes*, *Audio-visuelle Medien*, and study it carefully. The Goethe-Institut has produced a list of what it considers to be the most useful items with a short evaluation of each. Send to the Goethe-Institut* for this.

Hatfield Polytechnic German Centre

This offers a loan service and an interesting collection of dossiers on 'A' level topics, videos based on German television programmes **with worksheets** and audio-cassettes with notes. Hatfield Polytechnic*, like Brighton Polytechnic*, has specialised in video and audio.

The **Scottish Consultative Council on the Curriculum*** mounts initiatives in Scotland to produce materials and can inform you of what is available. Your own local authority may also have produced materials via working parties.

Using published teaching materials   19

MAGAZINES

Teachers of German are very fortunate to have **free** access to class sets of the excellent *Jugendmagazin* (formerly *Jugend-Scala*).

This is a high-quality, full colour magazine designed for German teenagers and foreign learners of German. It has lively features, pictures, games and can be selectively exploited as a teaching resource or simply made available for general interest reading.

A wonderful resource - and free! Just write to: Jugendmagazin, Vertrieb, Oberländer Ufer 180, Köln 51.

Jugendmagazin is published four times per year. With each class set of twenty magazines comes the accompanying magazine for teachers: *TIP*. This contains detailed suggestions from teachers on using the material in *Jugendmagazin*, some articles on teaching method in general and up-to-date background information on Germany.

Scala is available on a similar basis and is suitable for adults or 'A' level students.

You can obtain other free magazines from:

★ Bundeszentrale für gesundheitliche Aufklärung, Postfach 91 01 52, 5000 Köln 91 - these have various titles and deal with teenagers' problems in a lively style. Suitable age 15/16.

★ Bundeszentrale für politische Bildung, Berliner Freiheit 7, D 5300 Bonn 1 - suitable for 'A' level.

There is also a range of magazines in German produced in the UK for secondary school pupils by Mary Glasgow Publications: *Das Rad* (11-14; also a workbook and notes), *Schuß* (13-16), *Aktuell auf Deutsch* (15-18).

They appear six times per year and are lively and colourful. If your budget will not stretch that far, some pupils (or parents) may be persuaded to become subscribers themselves.

For more advanced learners there is *Authentik* produced by Trinity College Dublin. This consists of newspaper articles and radio news broadcasts presented in the form of a newspaper and cassettes with a learner's guide, a teacher's guide and a supplement containing exercises and tasks. It appears five times per year. Details from: Authentik, The O'Reilly Institute, Trinity College, Dublin 2. Tel: (010 353 1) 771512.

Presse und Sprache, published in Germany, is a similar compendium with suggested tasks. It appears monthly and is available from: Ellers & Schünemann Verlag, Postfach 10 60 67, 2800 Bremen 1, Germany.

COMPUTER SOFTWARE

Information technology has many applications in German teaching (see Chapters 4, 5 and 6). Look out for courses on CALL (Computer assisted language learning).

Authoring and word-processing packages offer you the chance to devise cloze, sequencing and other activities on texts which you type in yourself. Together with ready-made programs involving grammar exercises and vocabulary - sometimes with graphics (e.g. CUP's *Kopfjäger*) - they can help develop an awareness of the structures of German and at the very least provide entertaining reinforcement of work done in class. Simulations and role-plays will be popular also. ILECC* has recently produced *Now Read On* with authentic texts and reading tasks.

Probably the greatest opportunities for languages lie in the information-handling (database) and creative (word-processing) aspects.

Don't forget to check the compatibility of software and machines - BBC, Nimbus, etc. Read the CILT publication *Making the most of microcomputers* by Heather Rendall (1991) for practical advice on software.

Look at the pack *Learning languages with technology* (ed. Eric Brown) published by the National Centre for Educational Technology 1988. See also the CILT publication *Making the most of IT skills* by Sue Hewer (1989). There is a whole range of information published by NCET*, CILT* and NCCALL* at Ealing College of Higher Education*. Send to CILT for the NCET information sheets on *CALL*. These are regularly extended and updated. Ask for a list.

Many local authorities are developing policies for IT and modern languages. There may be a specialist advisory teacher in your authority who can assist you in keeping up to date with this fast-changing field.

SUMMARY

When evaluating the suitability of published materials for your students, it is important to take time to consider how they will help you to meet the objectives of your scheme of work and how they will motivate learners. Usually a core **structured** course augmented by materials designed specifically to develop particular **skills** and by resources designed to **interest** and **entertain** will produce the most effective mix. Within the constraints of your budget you should aim to give learners maximum access to books, audio tapes, video and magazines. Avoid if possible the two extremes of either investing **all** your funds in one expensive 'all-in' course book or inflicting 'death by a thousand worksheets'.

Sources of information:

Obtain all publishers' catalogues and, if possible, specimen copies, and seize any opportunity to look at materials at the Goethe-Institut* or in CILT's library.

Send to CILT* for information sheets on: publishers; bookshops; video materials; German courses for GCSE; German materials for a wide ability range; magazines; teaching materials for adults: German; vocational and business materials: German.

Best of all, visit the materials exhibition at the annual conference of ALL* (Association for Language Learning, formerly JCLA). There you will find almost **everything**!

Exploiting your own resources 4

Suchet, so werdet ihr finden.

What do you need and why?

Whatever books and tapes you acquire, there will always be a need for supplementary materials to provide extra practice in certain topic areas or skills, or indeed to fill any gaps in the coverage of your syllabus. This is where your random collection of realia and souvenirs from trips to Germany becomes important.

USING REALIA AND AUTHENTIC MATERIALS

Three general principles apply:

- Put a good piece of stimulus material to several uses, e.g. a menu can be used in a role-play or as a reading task.

- Where possible, let students handle the originals. This may mean laminating onto a card a particular piece **or** devising standard tasks which can be applied to any realia of a similar type if you have easy access to new supplies. Not everything has to be photocopied and turned into a worksheet.

- Don't be put off an attractive piece because it contains difficult grammar or structures. Ask yourself: can the students understand the main points, can they get the message, is it interesting? If so, use it, but make sure that any **tasks** you set are at the right level for your students.

Bits and pieces

If you have a box full of unsorted realia, let some students sort it under topic headings for you. This is an authentic reading task!

Groups could use some of the material to make collages with a theme (e.g. trip on the Rhine) using tickets, maps, advertisements, brochures, etc. They could then prepare an oral or written account of the events suggested by their collage. This lends itself to differentiated tasks: e.g. a) lists, b) diary in note form, c) connected account. The collages can be displayed on the walls when not in use.

Why not invent a detective story with realia as the clues?

Individual items of realia can be used also as a stimulus for a role-play or a range of other activities such as writing a response. The advantage of using them 'raw' is that little preparation time is involved and students become accustomed to the genuine articles.

Selecting authentic sources

When selecting authentic printed materials for more intensive exploitation, it is important to remember that interest, fun and relevance to the student are more important considerations than the topics, situations and settings of GCSE. The small print on the railway timetable may be specified by the GCSE syllabus and may even be relevant in real life, but how interesting is it to read? On the other hand, a funny or unusual newspaper item or cartoon which seems less relevant to the syllabus may teach the students far more. It is important to remember that the GCSE syllabuses are **testing** not **teaching** syllabuses and should not be allowed to take up all teaching and learning time. The best way to get good learning and results is to involve pupils in interesting and motivating activities.

From newspapers one can select items of permanent topicality - crime, social problems, incidents and accidents, human interest stories or local news.

With magazines, especially those aimed at a teenage market, there are the advice or agony column, the pen-friend page, reader's letters, horoscopes, stories, photo-stories and cartoons. These do not date quickly, neither do advertisements, recipes and television guides.

Music and fashion are trickier, but here the peer-group contrast is interesting and most students are aware of what was around a year or two ago anyway. Some personalities are very durable, even in the world of pop, and there is a sizeable nostalgia industry also.

A reading box which contains copies of special interest magazines on pets, cars, sport, etc has potential for developing the skill of extensive reading for those interested in the subject matter.

In addition to the well-known *Bravo*, *Popcorn*, etc, there is a range of magazines for slightly younger readers such as *Treff* and *Staffete*. The easiest way to get hold of those is via a school contact.

See 'Planning a reading programme' by M Buckby in *Developing modern language skills for GCSE*, Littlewood, W (ed), Nelson, 1989.

EXPLOITING THE MATERIALS

Here is a selection of ideas for different types of realia. Where possible, the task should be set in a realistic context and simulate what one really would do in that situation and with that text.

- ★ Advertisements
  - Identify key facts - price, colour, etc.
  - Choose products for a particular person or purpose. Say why.
  - Choose restaurant. Make arrangements.
  - What's on? Choose film, concert. Make arrangements.
  - At a higher level discuss the images of 'typical' life-styles.

- ★ Small advertisements
  - You are looking for something particular, is it here?
  - Write your own. Collect for class display.
  - Role-play: phone call based on item advertised for sale or jobs vacant or 'lonely hearts'.

- ★ Tourist/holiday brochures
  - Compare facilities and choose.
  - Write to confirm.
  - Plan activities for a week.
  - Role-play in the Information Office.

- ★ Forms
  - Ask questions and fill in details.
  - Telegram. Explaining to someone in full sentences what it says.

- ★ Letters/cards
  - Decipher handwriting. Copy out.
  - Summarise gist.
  - Reply.

- ★ Newspapers
  - Look for specific information, e.g. weather, sport.
  - Use headlines and pictures to select what to read.
  - Highlight key words and use these as a cue for telling someone what the article is about.

- ★ Menus
  - Role-plays. Discuss and decide order.
  - Explain items to a friend.

- ★ Recipes
  - Try it at home.
  - Give your own favourite recipe.
  - Shopping list.

- ★ Maps/town plans
  - Give and follow directions.
  - Tell a story/give an account of a trip.

- ★ School timetables/reports
  - Find out information from partner on lessons/times/days.
  - Fill in report on yourself.

- ★ Tickets/timetables
  - Information-gap role-plays.
  - Match passengers and lost tickets.
  - Plan a trip.
  - Reconstruct events.

- ★ TV/radio guides
  - Plan an evening's viewing.

- ★ Weather reports
  - Plan tomorrow's activities.
  - Explain forecast in simple terms.

When exploiting materials in this fashion try to involve as many **skills** as possible. Any authentic reading or listening item can be used for comprehension since it will by definition have an inherent **purpose**, i.e. a **message**, a

form and an **audience** (unlike a textbook passage which has probably been contrived to illustrate certain structures or vocabulary). Try to move on from comprehension to production.

Questions in English are not the only way to develop an understanding of the text. Extracting the essential information on to a grid or making a sun-diagram or flow chart based on the key words or ideas can all be done in German.

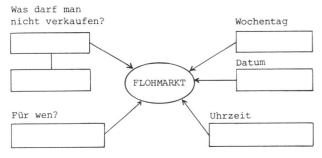

Deutsch Konkret (Langenscheidt, 1983)

True/false or matching up exercises can also be used in the first stage of this sequence. You could then have some oral or written exercises of a **mechanical** nature, i.e. concentrating on the forms of words or structures - substitution exercises; gap-filling; expanding cues or fragments into complete phrases. Role-plays with visual cues would come into this category. The next step could involve more open-ended role-plays with choices; changing the form of the text (e.g. a dialogue into a report or vice versa); summarising in the student's own words.

Finally, there should be a chance for students to use what they have learnt in order to express their own views or to construct an open-ended simulation. This process is even more effective if you can assemble a variety of text-types, for example on the theme of pocket-money:

★ Recorded interviews with young people.
★ Simulated discussion between young person and parent.
★ Statistics in a table or visual form - who gets what? - either from an authentic source or as a result of a class survey.
★ Magazine article.
★ Readers' letters.

See the *Übungstypologie* referred to in Chapter 3 for further ideas. Read also: Littlewood, W (ed) *Developing modern language skills for GCSE* (Nelson, 1989) and Klippel, F *Keep talking: communication fluency activities for language teaching* (CUP, 1985).

For more advanced learners consult the CILT* publication *German for 'A' level - a resource-based approach* (CILT, 1985). This contains many excellent suggestions.

LITERATURE AS A RESOURCE

One early misconception about the communicative approach was that it somehow excludes creative and imaginative language in favour of 'pure' information. The National Curriculum Working Group has stressed the importance of balancing objective and subjective uses of language. Indeed, authentic texts of an imaginative or literary nature have rarely been used pre-16, but there is every reason to seek ways of offering the right sort of materials to this age-group.

Popular paperback fiction for the younger teenager is one possibility. Another opportunity is provided by some recent anthologies of short literary texts, sometimes written by young people themselves, which have been published in Germany:

Märchen is an anthology of traditional and modern stories, accompanied by *Märchen, Aufgaben und Übungen*, a very lively book of parallel texts and tasks in the series *Literarische Texte im Unterricht* (Goethe-Institut, 1985/1986).

Junge deutsche Literatur is a collection of writings by young people (Goethe-Institut and Klett, 1989).

Two excellent anthologies are:

Lesen, na und? Ein literarisches Arbeitsbuch für die ersten Jahre Deutsch (Langenscheidt, 1987).

Lesespaß - Ein literarisches Materialienbuch für die ersten Jahre Deutsch (Langenscheidt, 1989).

Books from German publishers can be obtained through: The European Bookshop* and from Books in German*.

Next time you are in Germany, spend a little time searching for suitable short stories rather than filling yet another carrier bag with boring free handouts from the bank or station!

Stories can also be written by the students themselves, perhaps using well-known cartoon figures and speech bubbles. Other classes or younger students will provide a real-life audience for their efforts.

Poems can be very effective and require only simple language and syntax to make their point. Writing a poem, however simple, encourages initiative, creativity and awareness of the need to choose the right word.

Ein Tag
Der Wecker läutet.
Sie steht auf.
Es ist Morgen.
– Ich muß zur Schule – denkt sie.
Sie geht zur Schule.
Zuerst Algebra.
Meinetwegen.
Dann Französisch.
Ist ja egal!
Als nächstes Englisch – wie immer,
und dann Deutsch – na, und?
Als nächstes Geometrie – schon wieder?
Und zuletzt Musik.
Alles leer.
Sie geht nach Hause.
Sie ißt.
Dann macht sie Schulaufgaben.
Es ist Abend.
– Ich muß zu Bett – denkt sie.
Sie geht zu Bett.
Sie schläft.
Nein!
Sie weint.
Rosmarie (16)

Mein Tag
(Antwort für Rosmarie)
Der Wecker läutet.
Sie steht auf.
Es ist Morgen.
– Ich muß in die Küche – denkt sie.
Sie geht in die Küche.
Bereitet das Frühstück für all ihre Lieben.
Dann: Abwaschen, betten, abstauben wie immer.
Dann Bügeln.
Na, und?
Sie geht in die Küche, bereitet das Mittagessen.
Sie ißt.
Hört sich die Probleme der Kinder an.
Als nächstes abwaschen, flicken.
Schon wieder?
Zuletzt Musik.
Mit den Kindern zusammen.
Es ist später Abend.
Die Kinder gehen zur Ruhe.
Und sie?
Den Tisch decken für morgen.
Schuhe putzen.
Alles richten für den nächsten Tag.
– Ich muß nun zu Bett – denkt sie.
Sie geht zu Bett.
Sie ist müde.
Sie schläft.
Sie schläft ein mit der Hoffnung,
morgen wieder für alle da zu sein.
Wie immer.
Frau F. R. (46)

Deutsch Konkret (Langenscheidt, 1983)

COPYRIGHT

Some resources are designed to be copyright-free. Andrew Wright's book *1,000 pictures for teachers to copy* (Collins, 1984) is instant art, ideal for flash-cards and overhead transparencies. Others such as *Jugendmagazin*, which is in any case supplied free, and public information material from the *Bundesbahn* and *Bundespost*, or brochures and advertising material from commercial firms present no problem in practice.

The Goethe-Institut* publishes a list of German newspapers and magazines which have agreed to allow texts to be copied for teaching purposes. Indeed, there is no problem with this type of material providing you use it in the classroom only and do not seek to gain financially from it. Be warned, however, that if you wish to publish your efforts more widely you must ask permission. This is usually granted on texts but pictures can be a problem.

The Copyright Licensing Agency Ltd* (CLA) provides information on rules and regulations. Whoever is responsible for photocopiers in your educational institution should have that information. There is a special agreement which allows very limited duplication of material published in the UK. It is not worth illegally photocopying vast amounts of a book since it is usually cheaper in time and money to buy the original!

USING AUTHENTIC AUDIO, VIDEO, SATELLITE TV

Your contacts in Germany may be prepared to swap cassettes of radio and TV broadcasts (the systems are compatible) or you may have access to a 'dish' and satellite broadcasts in German. Send to CILT* for the information sheet on satellite TV and read the publication *Making the most of satellites and interactive video* by Brian Hill (CILT, 1991).

However you acquire this off-air material, it is a most valuable resource, not least because it establishes firmly in the minds of young learners the fact that German is used for real, everyday things like television and is not something obscure which you learn in school! In fact, although there are plenty of good techniques for exploiting authentic broadcasts, it is probably true to say that much of the value is achieved by the initial impact of a medium which aims to entertain. Advertisements, cartoons,

Sesamstraße, etc appeal to children (and adults) of all ages. Remember that they are designed for the widest possible audience including those with a limited command of language - or even a limited attention-span!

Radio commercials have everything. They have to, since most of their customers are doing something else at the time they hear them. Music, effects, repeated slogans, skillful voices all combine to hammer home the message in memorable fashion. What could be more communicative?

Typical tasks in ascending order of difficulty and descending order of importance would be:
What is the product? Perhaps give a choice of generic terms rather than brand-names, i.e. 'beer' rather than *Bischofs Premium Pilsener*.
Did you catch any claims about it? e.g. *frisch, rein*, etc.
What was the slogan? e.g. *Mon Chéri - wer kann dazu nein sagen?*
With TV commercials:
What looks different? food, house, clothes, etc. At a higher level the images of life-style and social roles in television commercials can be an excellent stimulus for discussion.

Real weather forecasts and traffic reports work better with a map - as on TV. For more advanced learners don't forget the German Language Service of the BBC*.

A popular science programme such as the *Knoff-Hoff Show* (ZDF) does scientific 'tricks' before a studio audience with such a strong visual impact that the words of the commentary serve simply to underline the key events and ideas. Programmes such as these are very accessible to near beginners and give them a real sense of achievement. After all, many Dutch children learn their German by watching German television programmes. Nevertheless, be conscious that too much **totally** unintelligible German will soon become discouraging and boring. Preparation of key words or ideas will pay dividends. For ways of doing this see the books which accompany the Thames TV series *Vidéothèque* and *Videothek*.

Action series, especially those which we know in the UK, will also be popular, although the novelty soon wears off. Many are too long for integration into a lesson and lose their point if you break them down into sections.

For ideas on using video and TV consult: *Making the most of video* by Brian Hill (CILT, 1989).

EQUIPMENT

As a result of GCSE, TVEI and other new approaches to language learning, it is important to communicate this message to Heads, Principals, Governors, PTAs, etc:

A foreign language is nowadays a practical subject.

You need a properly equipped subject base with **easy access** to as much as possible of the following:

★ **Overhead projector**. The visual impact of a presentation via an overhead transparency is very effective with learners of all ages and abilities.

★ **Good quality cassette players**. Use lots of treble. Remember many pupils have a degree of hearing impairment. Point the loudspeaker towards the class or have an external speaker fixed fairly high on the wall. Improve the acoustic of the room - insist on carpet.

★ **Headphones**. These can be used direct into a recorder or via a junction box so that perhaps four students can listen to a tape while other members of the class do something else.

★ **High speed cassette copier**. These are expensive but a good investment since they can copy both sides of a C60 cassette at one pass in under two minutes.

★ **Twin-deck cassette recorder with fast dubbing facility**. These are not so expensive. They are needed for editing master copies. At a pinch they can be used to copy cassettes for students although they are much slower than a high-speed copier.

★ **Individual cassettes for students**. Individual blank audio cassettes for the students are much cheaper to provide than one might expect and certainly cheaper than even the cheapest textbook. Almost all students have playback facilities at home and most will also be able to record speaking homeworks. Listening homework is a good idea as the student can hear an item as often as is needed. If you cannot afford bulk purchases of cassettes you can record onto the students' own cassettes which remain their property.

The Foreign Language Assistant can help you to produce your own recordings or you can compile suitable 'off-air' selections, news, weather, advertisements, etc.

If you are visited by a German exchange group make sure you record some live interviews. You could also record any native speakers living in your area and of course encourage classes to exchange audio or video cassettes with their German penfriends. When making your own recordings use the best quality microphone you can, preferably one with a uni-directional facility to eliminate over-intensive background noise.

★ **Television and video equipment**. With so much now available for German, these are essential. If you have access to a video **camera** it is very motivating for students to plan and record their own role-plays and interviews. Read Jack Lonergan's book *Making the most of your video camera* (CILT, 1990) for some excellent ideas.

★ **Computer system**. You should have access to a network and preferably your own free-standing computer for practice. The various applications of Information Technology will become more important with the advent of the National Curriculum.

Make your case for investment in these facilities by showing senior management and governors that you know how to use them to meet the new educational and vocational objectives of foreign language learning. Think through and attempt to cost also the storage and security implications.

A properly argued and professionally produced submission for hardware often appeals to school management or the LEA and can attract sponsorship from commercial organisations.

Find out more by reading:

Little, D, S Devitt and D Singleton *Learning foreign languages from authentic texts: theory and practice.* CILT (1989)

Littlewood, W (ed) *Developing modern language skills for GCSE.* Nelson (1989)

Übungstypologie zum kommunikativen Deutschunterricht. Langenscheidt (1981)

Jugendliteratur im kommunikativen Deutschunterricht. Langenscheidt (1985)

Technology in Language Learning - a series of six titles from CILT:
- *Making the most of video* by Brian Hill (1989)
- *Making the most of IT skills* by Sue Hewer (1989)
- *Making the most of your video camera* by Jack Lonergan (1990)
- *Making the most of audio* by Anthony Barley (1990)
- *Making the most of micro-computers* by Heather Rendall (1991)
- *Making the most of satellites and interactive video* by Brian Hill (1991)

German for 'A' level - a resource-based approach. CILT (1985)

CILT information sheets:
Literature in foreign language teaching: some sources for 'A' level and *'A' level teaching materials: German.*

di Pietro, R *Strategic interaction.* CUP (1987)

Ur, P *Discussions that work.* CUP (1981)

Jones, B *Using authentic resources in teaching French.* CILT (1984)

CILT Pathfinder Series: *Reading for pleasure in a foreign language* by Ann Swarbrick (1990).

Teaching and learning styles 5

Zu den Füßen eines Lehrers sitzen.

CHANGING NEEDS

We live in a time of rapid change in society as a whole and in education in particular. This does not mean that only what is new is true, but it does mean that the way you teach and the way you learn must take account of changes in the needs and demands of individuals, of society and of the world of work.

The major factors affecting teachers of German from beginners to 'A' level include:

★ a new emphasis on practical communication, bearing in mind that effective communication requires a good understanding of the cultural background;

★ individual needs and **personal** language - the communicative approach;

★ new examination syllabuses and National Curriculum attainment targets;

★ the entitlement of **all** to experience a foreign language, to enjoy the experience and to succeed at it;

★ the vocational needs of students and the demands of industry and commerce;

★ changing objectives and expectations in education in general.

What are the practical implications?

Classes

Mixed ability classes or sets by ability? A long-running ideological dispute. The DES in effect backs setting by ability groupings after a diagnostic year (*Modern languages in the school curriculum,* 1988; *Curriculum Matters 8,* 1987). Your school may have a different policy.

- **Be pragmatic**. Even within sets there is often a wide range of aptitudes - although not as wide as in a mixed-ability class.

- **Motivation** is probably more important than ability - but see the section on Special Educational Needs below.

- Whatever your situation, it makes sense to **differentiate** for learners at varying stages of development. Techniques to cope with mixed-ability classes are therefore good practice in any type of class, including 'A' level and adult education classes.

DIFFERENTIATION

This means having different objectives and activities for different students or groups of students and can be achieved by variations on three basic approaches. It applies both to teaching and assessing or testing. It is most easily implemented by careful planning of homework tasks but must also be practised during lessons.

- All do the same task but you expect different things from different students, e.g. in whole class oral work you ask a question such as:

Was habt ihr übers Wochenende gemacht?

From Student A you accept *Hausaufgaben und schwimmen*, but with Student B you insist on *Meine Freundin und ich sind schwimmen gegangen*. This is known as differentiation by outcome.

- Have a sequence of tasks which allows the less able to achieve something that makes sense and yet offers the more able further activities to develop their skills, e.g.

For Student A:
Read this entertainments guide and choose something you would like to see.

For Student B:
Do the same and also leave a note in German for your friend saying where you are going and when.

Of course Student A might want to go on to the further task - in which case you provide extra help. (You can still differentiate by outcome when you assess the notes they have written.)

Open-ended tasks can be useful. For example, 'Listen to the tape and note starting and finishing times in the grid. Note down other relevant details you catch.'

- Choose different tasks for groups or individuals. A group task can be based on different input, i.e. reading or listening, and could require different levels of contribution to the same end product, ranging from lists or illustrations to written-up reports. This can lead to putting together the results of a number of tasks for the whole group or class in order to form a worthwhile whole, such as the solution to a problem. This is known as the 'jigsaw' approach. A gently guided choice can ensure that students do not take on too much or too little.

Your **scheme of work** should also differentiate objectives between ability sets or for levels of ability within a class.

- The simplest and most flexible way to do this is to identify a **core** or basic level of knowledge, skills and activities for a **unit** which all students should aim for and then specify further levels and further objectives for the average and above-average. This enables different sets or all the pupils within one set to move from one unit (or topic) to the next at the same time and is practical in terms of whole-class teaching, organisation of resources and monitoring and assessing progress. Providing you have differentiated your teaching as suggested, you will avoid the main pitfall of the 'lock-step' approach which is to aim at the middle and move forward before some are ready, while others have long been marking time. (See Chapter 8.)

TEACHING FROM THE FRONT

The traditional way of imparting information to a class is still very effective in the right circumstances. A dynamic presentation of new material assisted by visual aids, with lots of German from the teacher to reinforce the main points and with all members of the class involved, gives impetus and pace to a lesson.

There is an interesting example in the video *The communicative classroom* (BBC Education* Inset). Make sure you obtain and read the accompanying teacher's notes.

Perhaps the greatest danger in frontal teaching is that by the end of the lesson the teacher has talked non-stop and the learners have contributed almost nothing. If the teacher talk is in German this can at least be characterised as listening input - providing the listeners are **participating** in some way, perhaps via an active listening task such as checking off information heard on a grid, or making a real choice based on what they hear.

For more ideas see P Ur *Teaching listening comprehension* (CUP, 1984) and S Rixon *Developing listening skills* (Macmillan, 1986).

GROUP-WORK

This can achieve other objectives such as the skills of planning and cooperating. It does need very careful organisation of resources to ensure that each member of a group has something to do and that all understand the task. See the section on differentiation above.

PAIR-WORK

Active learning roles are especially important for boys (see HMI report *Boys and modern languages,* DES, 1985). Pair-work is very convenient for practising and consolidating structures via dialogues and role-plays. It means that everyone speaks and can gain confidence before perhaps being required to perform to the teacher or to the rest of the class.

Writing, reading or listening tasks can also benefit from a cooperative approach.

With younger learners especially it is vital to make the task clear and quite short. Insist on **German only** while the pair-work is taking place.

Walk around steadily, listening briefly and unobtrusively to everyone practising. This keeps them on their toes and enables you to identify any **serious** errors which can be corrected **afterwards**.

ERRORS

Distinguish between errors which obscure communication and those which don't.

sein- Schwester = grammatical error
seine Schwester = communicative error - if the speaker meant to say *ihre Schwester!*

Choosing the wrong pronoun, using the wrong tense, giving offence perhaps by using *du* instead of *Sie* are typical 'communicative' errors. These need to be corrected - but without discouraging the student or inhibiting fluency, especially in class oral work.

Everyone makes mistakes when first trying to apply knowledge in practice and although one wants to streamline the process when acquiring a second language, most learners will need their quota of *Annäherungsversuche* before they assimilate a new structure.

GRAMMAR

Did language teachers get it all wrong for centuries? Has grammar been abolished? Obviously not.

Ungrammatical language does not communicate effectively. Grammatical competence is a part of communicative competence. Some have misinterpreted the communicative basis of GCSE as meaning that students need not develop any formal grammatical competence. Look again at the National Criteria and at the syllabuses.

A communicative approach is pragmatic, there is no single **right** way and nothing is taboo. If it interests the learner and assists learning then it is appropriate. Many will start to learn inductively via practice and observation of usage. Point out patterns in German and compare/contrast with English usage. Where necessary, rationalise with rules and exceptions. Only an approach which **starts** with grammatical exposition and paradigms is **un**communicative.

COMMUNICATIVE ACTIVITIES

Whether it is attempted in the world outside the classroom, in a class, in a group, in pairs or as an individual task, a **communicative** or **real-life** activity has certain characteristics:

What is said is more important than how it is said. Content, message is more important than form - and probably unpredictable. There is a reason: an information gap to be filled, a problem solved, a decision reached, a contact made. Most important of all, there is an element of personal choice and creativity.

Compare this with traditional oral work in class:

What is to be said is decided by textbook and teacher and is predictable and often pointless, e.g. *Wie ist das Wetter heute?* Students can sometimes answer questions without understanding them since the emphasis is on the form not the content. One person (teacher) already knows the answers to the questions he is putting to the class.

There are some excellent collections of communicative activities and games. Particularly recommended is:

Developing communication skills - a practical handbook for language teachers with examples in English, French and German by Pat Pattison (CUP, 1987).

There is no mystique about communicative activities - in fact quite the opposite since they mirror everyday life. You can easily transform a traditional oral drill into a communicative activity by introducing an element of **unpredictability** or by establishing a **need to know**.

For example:
★ Textbook shopping dialogue with list of prices given.

- Pupils make their own secret lists of prices. Others have to find out which shop is cheapest for certain items or cheapest overall.

★ General interrogation about hobbies and interests.

- Pupils do a class survey of most popular hobbies or find out who watches *Neighbours*, find out who doesn't like it and can say why.

There are commercially available collections of information-gap role-plays in German with separate pages or books for Partner A and

Partner B. Alternatively, you can construct your own materials based on *Developing communication skills* (see above) or on Andrew Wright's book *1000 pictures for teachers to copy* (Collins, 1984).

Don't forget communicative **writing,** i.e. for a real **audience,** e.g. stories for younger learners, small ads for classroom 'exchange and mart', class exchange of letters, class magazine.

INDEPENDENT LEARNING

Self-supported study allows infinite differentiation and the opportunity to negotiate a learning programme with each student. It enables the student to learn to organise work and find things out. The teacher helps when needed and provides or negotiates with the students the framework of resources, projects and targets. **Independent** learning is not necessarily **individual** learning. Students can work in groups.

This approach is fundamental to such schemes as FLAW and BTEC (see Chapter 2) but it has advantages for all learners, even beginners. For some teachers it is the normal procedure in lessons, with the class brought together for discussion or input as the exception rather than the rule.

Even within a more conventional approach to teaching there are opportunities for having different activities happening simultaneously in the classroom: perhaps pupils at one table are preparing a role-play, at another they are designing a poster, at another doing a listening comprehension via headsets and so on. At the very least, a class collection of reading material which pupils select from or work through at their own rate will help develop some independent study skills. Sessions for individuals at the computer can provide reinforcement and support - and often reveal hidden talents.

There are, of course, major implications for the provision and organisation of resources. On the one hand, you can make full use of odd copies of various books, worksheets and realia. On the other hand, you will need to have headsets for listening and possibly recording facilities for oral work. You also need to plan very carefully so that you can devote your time to helping, advising or monitoring individuals or groups.

ORGANISING THE CLASSROOM

The traditional layout of desks is not conducive to group work or any more flexible teaching style.

Try these instead:

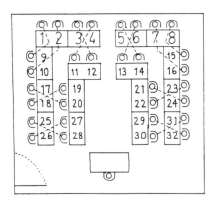
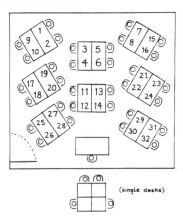

Developing communications skills by Pat Pattison (CUP, 1987)

Other variations are possible. This one enables the teacher to tutor small groups.

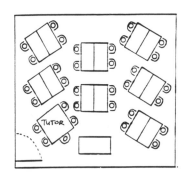

Making the most of your video camera by Jack Lonergan (CILT, 1990)

DRAMA AND MUSIC

Why not turn those boring role-plays into mini-productions (perhaps on video) with props, actors and producer, a critical audience awarding ratings for technical proficiency and artistic merit and, above all, elements of the unexpected and humorous? Any 'normal' language activity can be enhanced by the addition of this personal and creative dimension.

Why not let a tune help you memorise the words? *Eine Kleine Deutschmusik* (Langenscheidt, 1983) sets dialogues and useful phrases to well-known tunes. Try this to the tune of *Mein Hut, der hat drei Ecken*:

> *Geht dieser Zug nach Frankfurt?*
> *Nein, nein, der geht nach Trier.*
> *Wann geht ein Zug nach Frankfurt?*
> *Um fünfzehn Uhr, Gleis vier.*

For further ideas read: A Duff and A Malley *Drama techniques in language learning* (CUP, 1978).

THE TECHNOLOGICAL AND VOCATIONAL APPROACH

The 'TVEI' approach to the curriculum promotes skills and ways of learning which reflect the demands of the world of work. It also promotes the use of technology, particularly information technology. Remember that IT is a means to an end and that it can be used to enhance learning directly or indirectly in many everyday situations. Look for ways in which students can develop an IT capability through language learning.

The implications for learning German would include:

- cross-curricular links, e.g. with business studies;
- a task-based approach with specific goals and assignments, e.g. design a brochure in German to advertise the attractions of the home town or area;
- continuous assessment, self-evaluation and profiling;
- independent study and research;
- exchange of information - perhaps via electronic mail;
- foreign visits including industrial visits or work experience;
- use of technology - recording, word-processing, using or creating a database.

The idea is not to train students for a specific job but to enable them to learn the skills employers need:

- to be confident and effective communicators;
- to show initiative;
- to work cooperatively;
- to find out information;
- to utilise resources.

One implication for your teaching objectives would be to stress the students' role as **providers** of the service, e.g. receptionist, tourist guide, to German-speaking customers rather than as consumers/tourists themselves. Being polite/using the accepted formulae, answering enquiries, explaining, apologising in German are all very practical things to learn.

Doing written tasks on a word-processor or creating a database of vocabulary on a computer are very motivating activities. The results of a class survey, for example, can be displayed using pie charts and graphs. Don't forget that students will be acquiring these IT skills in primary schools as part of the National Curriculum and that their skills will be quite sophisticated by secondary level. There is also an important equal opportunities aspect - technology for girls and active real-life language tasks for boys - which challenges the traditional image of foreign language learning.

Look at the *Foreign languages in tourism* package produced by Kate Corney, available from North Yorkshire Language Centre, Park Grove, York, Y03 7ED, which is based on these principles, and at *Willkommen bei V.A.G.* from Hodder & Stoughton.

SPECIAL EDUCATIONAL NEEDS

As German is taught increasingly to pupils of all abilities 11-16, this issue comes to the fore. Fortunately, if your approach is both **communicative** and **differentiated** (see above) you have a good chance of making your German course accessible. Information Technology also has much to offer these pupils. 'Special needs' could encompass a fair proportion of any class, ranging through those with reading difficulties, with hearing impairment or with marked aptitudes. It does not simply mean 'low attainers'. Discuss these issues with the Special Needs Department in your school.

Some typical strategies for language teachers:

- clear, short-term goals with rewards. Display work in the classroom;

- core and extended worksheets and homeworks;

- think carefully how you can explain and demonstrate a task clearly;

- pupils work in pairs and groups where possible;

- support **listening** with visual cues and hold attention with active tasks, e.g. listen out for these names of people or things and point at them when you hear them;

- give optional extra clues, e.g. answers in jumbled order on the other side of the sheet for those who need help;

- role-plays: practise by putting each statement on a card and asking students to put them together in the right order as they say them;

- record model phrases and structures on cassette for individuals to take home for extra practice;

- train students to identify **signposts** in reading texts - headlines, captions;

- underline or extract and enlarge key sections;

- avoid overuse of English either in rubrics or in tasks, i.e. avoid requiring sentence answers in English. Go instead for grids, matching up words and pictures, tick or cross. **Direct** response avoids the hurdle of conceptualising and producing a sentence;

- gap-filling, perhaps via a computer program such as *Developing tray* (ILECC*). A computer can make even repetitive and mechanical exercises more interesting, but programs such as *Developing tray* go much further than this and stimulate an awareness of syntax and important language skills such as prediction;

- when copying, pupils should work from a sheet or book beside them rather than from the board;

- use the word-processor to write notes, messages, lists and to re-draft work;

- avoid over-crowded worksheets, dark colours and very small print. Put space around words and use bold graphical devices (boxes, arrows, etc).

As with mixed-ability strategies, this approach starts from a common-sense analysis of the needs of the learner. As a general principle this holds for all types of learner at all levels.

Himmel und Hölle

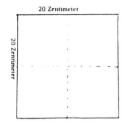 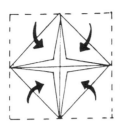  

1. *Das Blatt entlang der gestrichelten Linien falten!*

2. *Die Rückseite nach oben drehen und die Ecken zur Mitte umklappen!*

3. *Das gefaltete Blatt umdrehen und die Ecken wieder zur Mitte umklappen!*

4. *Die Mitte eindrücken! Man kann jetzt die Figur beschriften.*

    Außen - *die Zahlen*
    Innen - *Symbole für die Ortsangaben*
    Unten - *Symbole für die Wegbeschreibung*

5. *Zum Spielbeginn die Finger beider Hände in die Höhlen stecken und die vier Ecken so zusammenschließen, daß nur die Zahlen sichtbar sind.*

Spielverlauf

A: *Eins, zwei, drei usw.*

B: *Entschuldigung! Wie komme ich am besten zum Bahnhof?*

A: *Sie nehmen die erste Straße links und dann geradeaus.*

B: *Erste Straße links und dann geradeaus. Vielen Dank.*

A: *Nichts zu danken. Auf Wiedersehen!*

B: *Auf Wiedersehen!*

Das Spiel kann immer wieder von neuem gespielt werden, bis die Wegangaben nach allen Orten erfragt worden sind.

Die Schüler können die Rollen tauschen, so daß jeder einmal fragt und einmal antwortet.

Communication re-activated: teaching pupils with learning difficulties by Bernardette Holmes (CILT, 1991)

LANGUAGE AWARENESS

This is sometimes taught as a separate course or module but some aspects can be integrated. For example:

- recognition of common 'Germanic' vocabulary: *Tür Tochter Apfel* - recognise the word despite the spelling. 'Guessing rules' for changing consonants;

- recognise common words with different usage: *Fleisch Stuhl Schwein*;

- compare Latin or Greek root words in English with Germanic versions: material - *Stoff*; environment - *Umwelt*; television - *Fernsehen*;

- 'international' words, loan words;

- look at a language map of Europe and discuss the history of language.

Find out more by reading *Awareness of language - an introduction* by Eric Hawkins (CUP, 1987).

USE OF THE FOREIGN LANGUAGE AND USE OF THE MOTHER TONGUE IN THE CLASSROOM

In a class, such as is often found in EFL teaching, where students do not share a common mother tongue, it is sensible to conduct all exchanges in the target language. Sometimes this situation is found in foreign language classes in schools or colleges.

Nevertheless, the mother tongue or 'preferred language' of most students of German in the UK will be English. What is the role of English in the foreign language class? Should German be the only language used in the German class?

USE GERMAN AS MUCH AS POSSIBLE

- time is precious. Students need the maximum listening input;

- the sounds and intonation of the language are absorbed subliminally;

- it is especially important to give all instructions and messages in German as soon as possible, since this establishes in younger monolingual minds the notion that another language can be used for real communication;

- students will learn to get the gist of what is said;

- coping for a period of time entirely in German gives the student a sense of achievement;

- it's the next best thing to being in Germany.

WHEN IS THERE A CASE FOR USING ENGLISH?

- to explain and negotiate objectives and means of achieving them in the early stages of a course;

- when learners do not understand what they are to do and why;

- when they wish to pursue a point or interest beyond their level of competence in German;

- when they want to consolidate and rationalise what they are learning - often by comparison with structures in their own language;

- when you wish to encourage and reassure those less resilient learners for whom blanket use of the target language is a complete culture-shock and turn-off;

- for some assessment and testing.

CONSIDER

- penfriends often use both languages in the same letter, exchange pupils converse in either or both simultaneously. In fact, communication is often effectively carried out by each person using his/her own native language;

- the audio-lingual, pattern drill approach used the foreign language all the time - but structures were simply imitated and meaning or 'messages' were irrelevant;

- a communicative approach starts from the experience and needs of the learner, who does not pretend to be German or assume a new 'neutral' identity;

- research into the experience of **bilingual** children shows that they learn most effectively when helped to relate the **new** language to the structures and usage of their **first** language and culture. Total immersion in the second language disorientates them and inhibits communication.

For further thoughts on this read *The use of English in the foreign language classroom* by M Buckby in York Papers in Language Teaching (1985 - LTC, University of York).

Use German as much as you possibly can and reflect on missed opportunities to do so - would they have understood, how could you have helped by rephrasing, using cognates, using mimic and gesture, by using visual support?

As with all the teaching techniques discussed in this chapter, there is always room for improvement and one can only try to do better next time...!

Find out more by reading:

Pattison, P *Developing communication skills - a practical handbook.* CUP (1987)

Wright, A, D Betteridge, M Buckby *Games for language learning.* CUP (1984)

Lohfert, W *Kommunikative spiele für Deutsch als Fremdsprache.* Hueber Verlag (1983)

Müller, M, I Werteneschlag, J Wolff *Autonomes und partnerschaftliches Lernen.* Langenscheidt (1989)

Hewer, S *Making the most of IT skills.* CILT (1989)

Johnstone, R *Communicative interaction: a guide for language teachers.* CILT (1989)

CILT information sheet: *What is meant by a communicative approach to language teaching?*

Gathercole, I (ed) *Autonomy in language learning.* CILT (1990)

CILT Pathfinder Series:

Halliwell, S, B Jones *On target - teaching in the target language.* CILT (1991)

Holmes, B *Communication re-activated - teaching pupils with learning difficulties.* CILT (1991)

Halliwell, S *Yes - but will they behave? - Managing the interactive classroom.* CILT (1991)

Bringing the country into the class   6

Die Müh' ist klein, der Spaß ist groß.

Why?

- to narrow the gap between the classroom and the real world;
- to give students an impression of country and people;
- to promote cultural awareness and understanding;
- to enliven lessons and the learning environment.

THE GERMAN ASSISTANT

If you do not have an assistant make the case to your institution for employing one. They can be of immense value:

to **students**
- ★ by providing an opportunity for them to communicate with a real live native German speaker;
- ★ by enabling them to have more individual conversation practice and a change of teaching style.

to **teachers**
- ★ by sharing the task of assessing pupils' spoken performance;
- ★ as a model and a resource for maintaining and improving your own skills;
- ★ by working either with you in class or by taking small groups of pupils for intensive practice for exams;
- ★ as a source of authentic materials.

Both GCSE and 'A' level give high priority to speaking and listening and to native speakers as models for both students and teachers. Pupils are at a **disadvantage** if they have no access to FL assistants.

The assistants scheme is administered nationally by the Central Bureau for Educational Visits and Exchanges* but it is the responsibility of the LEA or school to appoint and provide in-service support. It is also important to involve the Assistant in the social life of the school or area.

The Goethe-Institut* is a valuable resource for them and has produced (1989) a handbook of information and practical tips. The Central Bureau provides advice also.

See also:

The German assistant's handbook, (available from ALL*)
The handbook for the foreign assistant by Sam Muir (MGP, 1975)
Using the foreign language assistant from the National Association of Language Advisers and the Central Bureau (available from ALL*)

CLASS-TO-CLASS LINKS

Setting up a link with a school in Germany can ensure a steady stream of letters, letter-cassettes and various realia. If your school has a pupil exchange scheme with a German school, this is a way of involving everyone in the contact rather than simply those who are able to take part in an exchange visit. It can also prepare the ground for an exchange either for an individual or for an institution.

Borough or town twinning arrangements are the easiest point of initial contact (there may even be access to funding for this). Consult the Central Bureau* about setting up a twinning scheme and, in your LEA, ask your local Adviser. In practice, there is never any problem in establishing class-to-class or penfriend links with German schools.

36 GERMAN

Tips

Pupils could:
- write half the letter in German and half in English, thus providing reading and writing practice for both sides;
- send photos and excerpts from magazines about hobbies, music, fashions;
- introduce themselves on a cassette;
- record a cassette on a theme or topic and ask the German school to respond.

ELECTRONIC MAIL

Just as recording a cassette to send to someone 'for real' can be very motivating, so can the transmission and receipt of information via the latest technology. Finding a message from a German school in your electronic mailbox and sending a response gives a new meaning to reading and writing! Many institutions in Germany are already linked in to a system which we can access via Campus 2000. Send to CILT for the information sheet on *CILT online information*.

CLASSROOM DISPLAYS

Encourage pupils to make their own displays or selections of realia from material collected on trips abroad. The displays could be changed to fit the topics being studied currently.

Signs and notices such as *Ausgang, Vorsicht!* etc can be produced by the pupils.

Posters, collages of colourful pictures from magazines, postcards - displays of the pupils' own work - a class newspaper in German - cards and letters received from the 'exchange' school - cartoons - calendars - picture vocabulary: all these create a natural context and cheerful ambience for using German.

Items such as bottles, labels, packets, clothes, etc can add life to role-plays. This is an area where the Assistant can be very useful. In some classrooms it may be feasible to set up a shop with various goods and prices on display.

DIALECTS AND SONGS

One way to bring the language alive is to let students hear a variety of dialects, perhaps by listening to traditional and modern songs. *Spider Murphy Gang* (bayerisch), *De Höhner* (kölsch) and *Hannes Wader* (plattdeutsch) are good examples.

See if your students can translate this traditional song from Niederdeutsch into High German and into English:

Over de stillen Straten
geit klar de Klockenslag
Good Nacht, lot uns nu slapen
Un morgen is ok een Dag.

German is after all not a remote language...!

For songs and texts in dialect, start by consulting the Goethe-Institut*.

SLIDES, FILMS, VIDEOS, POSTERS

Inter Nationes* and the Goethe-Institut* have a wide range of resources showing the regions of Germany, cities, people, customs, music, etc. Send to CILT for the information sheet on: *Sources of posters, maps and wallcharts*.

Some of these images of Germany may well arouse the curiosity and stir the imagination especially of younger learners. Try to ensure a balanced picture, however, i.e. not all *Fachwerkhäuser* and mountains.

Naturally enough, the tourist offices of the German-speaking countries and the brochures of the travel companies will emphasise the tourist attractions - and why not? - but it is important that the visual images pupils receive do reflect also the highly industrialised and highly developed nature of those societies. Discuss with pupils what impression of these countries they have gained from the British media and discuss whether it contrasts with their own experience, with what they have learned from meeting the German Assistant and with what they have learned from corresponding with German pupils.

Deutsch Konkret (Langenscheidt, 1983)

School travel and exchange visits 7

Wenn jemand eine Reise tut,
So kann er was erzählen.

One advantage of the communicative approach with its emphasis on authentic materials and realistic tasks, is that young people should be better prepared both linguistically and culturally for that first visit.

Nevertheless, there is often a problem for the junior tourist, particularly in the more popular holiday areas. The well-known enthusiasm of the Germans to use their English, however limited or imperfect, can easily demoralise the youngster who is gathering courage to carry out a transaction in a shop or a bank. Adults in this position may be able to explain that they wish to practise and improve a beginner's command of German and insist on establishing an equal relationship which preserves the self-respect of both parties. This defensive strategy is not so easily employed by a young person; it should therefore be taught and practised.

If visiting these tourist areas, talk about the problem in advance and put it into perspective by explaining the reasons for it. Discuss the social and practical advantages of making contact with Germans in German.

Better still, plan visits where contact is not limited to the realm of obtaining goods and services from the natives and where pupils will quickly find out that it is anyway not true that 'they all speak English'.

GROUP TOURS TO GERMANY

School travel companies offer general interest tours by coach, usually for seven days, and often to the Rhineland or the Mosel. Both destinations are within one day's range of the channel ports for a coach with one driver.

These tours represent reasonable value for money and are quite popular. Their educational value is limited but they are a reassuring introduction to the country for those young learners who would not yet have the confidence to stay with a German family.

Some companies offer language courses on these package tours with assignments and worksheets based on the local area. Such courses can work very well and at least ensure that students keep their eyes open and take note of their surroundings. Speaking tasks also establish the practical uses of the language in the learners' minds and help to build their confidence, e.g. find out where the cinema is, order something to drink in a cafe, ask where the toilets are.

Major firms offering these packages send their brochures to schools as a matter of course.

Consult colleagues in other schools also and benefit from their experience.

HOME STAYS

These constitute in effect a package tour with accommodation as paying guests in a German family. This is not an exchange since there is no reciprocal arrangement.

Contact: SEE Europe Limited, 45 Church Street, Weybridge, Surrey KT13 8DG or Euro-Academy Outbound, 77a George Street, Croydon CR0 1LD for further information.

MORE ADVANCED COURSES

More extensive courses either for individuals or for groups are offered by the Goethe-Institut*. Details either from your 'local' branch or direct from the Goethe-Institut*, München.

The Anglo-Austrian Society, Austrian Institute* has a programme of language courses, home stays and exchanges.

The Central Bureau* publishes complete guides and full information on all aspects of educational visits and exchanges. Ask for *Study holidays and Working holidays*. The Schools Unit of the Central Bureau provides a full advice service to the schools sector on developing international links and exchanges.

DAAD (*Deutscher Akademischer Austauschdienst*) publishes a list of holiday courses at all levels held in German technical colleges and universities. Contact: German Academic Exchange Service, 11-15 Arlington Street, London SW1.

EXCHANGES

Potentially the most valuable form of educational travel. If you do not have a personal contact with a teacher in a German school there are two ways of establishing a link.

- Contact the Central Bureau* (see above). To say that you will have no problem in finding a suitable partner school is an understatement! Unfortunately, it remains true that there are more German institutions enthusiastically seeking contact with us than there are willing partners for them in the UK.

- Contact your local council and enquire about twinning arrangements with a town in Germany. These contacts are often under-exploited by councils and you may obtain some financial support.

WORK EXPERIENCE

Ask your LEA Adviser if there are any local schemes for work experience for older students. At the lowest level this could simply involve a day visit to an office or factory as part of a normal exchange trip or school journey. It could involve an individual student helping out in a firm for a week or two. The benefits to that student would be enormous. Seek help in ascertaining the insurance situation where proper work experience is involved.

The European Community and the Department of Employment are backing the European Work Experience project (EWE) which has been set up to advise and make contacts for sixth-formers and other young people pursuing vocational training. Information from: UK Lingua Unit, Seymour Mews House, Seymour Mews, London W1H 9PE.

German firms have shown a willingness to recruit British youngsters of high ability who have done a period of work experience in Germany.

TIPS ON RUNNING SCHOOL JOURNEYS

- Target specific groups of pupils and ensure that any programme of activities is suitable and enjoyable. Look also at the possibility of involving the football team, the choir, or other groups, whether or not they are learning German.

- Try to involve colleagues who are experienced in organising trips abroad.

- Work out a diary of what you need to do and when, e.g.:

    - obtain school and LEA permission;
    - check DES guidelines, school and LEA policy on charging for trips in or out of school hours;
    - check what individual financial assistance or grants may be available;
    - check likely clashes with other school journeys or activities;
    - check dates when deposits and full payment are required;
    - check passport requirements well in advance. If travelling on individual passports ask to see them to check validity and possible visa complications. Insist on seeing individual E111s also (i.e. reciprocal EC arrangement for medical attention - forms from DHSS office);
    - give yourself a wide safety margin when costing any trip - even an 'inclusive' package deal;
    - plan comprehensive insurance cover. Contact the School Journey Association* or check scope of cover offered by tour operator;
    - if organising your own travel think carefully about the comparative costs and convenience of travel by coach, rail or air.

Contact: **Touropa**, (German Student Travel Service), 52 Grosvenor Gardens, London SW1 (071-730 2101).

Transalpino Limited, 71-75 Buckingham Palace Road, London SW1 (071-834 9656).

School travel and exchange visits

GTF (German Tourist Facilities Limited) - especially for cheap flights - 184 Kensington Church Street, London W8 4DP (071-229 2474).

Dragons International - for coach travel - The Old Vicarage, South Newington, Banbury, Oxon OX15 4JN (0295 721717).

- Having decided on the purpose, dates and cost of your trip, advertise it to your potential customers via slides or other visual material and explanations in class. Summarise all important information and conditions very clearly on the first letter plus reply slip to parents.

- Check applicants' suitability with other colleagues!

- Take payment by instalments. Set the deposit at a level which will not deter the committed but will deter the frivolous. Set a clear date for final settlement - this should be in advance of that required by the travel company.

- Hold a meeting for everybody involved, sufficiently in advance of departure date for last minute problems to be resolved.

- Lay down the law very clearly about the standards you expect. Show parents slides and pictures and give a general outline of activities and perhaps times when pupils will not be directly supervised. Explain details of insurance cover. Invite questions and discussion to clarify any worries.

- After the meeting summarise all the points made and details of final arrangements in a letter to all participants.

- In general: double check all arrangements before the departure date, keep the School Secretary informed of all arrangements and keep all bills and receipts to assist accounting procedures.

- Make sure the Head and Governors are aware of what you are doing **voluntarily** on behalf of them and the pupils. Invite them to the meetings before and after the trip, mount displays of photos, souvenirs, pupils' work and impressions. Best of all invite them along - then they also have a stake in the success of your venture.

PLANNING AN EXCHANGE

The Central Bureau* may fund a study visit to help set up a well planned exchange. A close understanding with the organiser at the German end is essential to success.

- Agree criteria for pairing pupils. The original letter to parents should include a form to fill in specifying interests, brothers and sisters, etc. This could be in both languages.

- A separate form with address, emergency contact numbers, medical conditions, etc is also essential for your records.

- Ensure everyone understands that it is the quality of the welcome that counts - not the standard of accommodation. Agree details such as: hosts pay for outings but guest pays for presents, souvenirs, snacks, etc.

- Agree how many days partners are to spend in school together. Discuss group outings. Who pays? Should any particular outing be for guests only?

- Ensure hosts and guests have the same detailed programme and perhaps everybody's address and telephone numbers so that small groups can cooperate amongst themselves during free time.

SUMMARY

- When planning a trip consult experienced colleagues and if possible take someone experienced with you.

- Look very carefully at insurance cover.

- Contact your union or professional association for advice about the latest regulations - remember a consent form signed by a parent may indemnify the LEA but not you. Similarly, do not expect a tour operator to point out any financial or legal hazards.

- Insist on maximum support and consideration from your school or college. The institution's image is considerably enhanced by well planned and well run educational visits.

Everyone benefits - students, parents, school - make sure you and your department gain too. Enjoy the gratitude and increased motivation of your pupils - you will have earned it!

GERMAN

What we learnt in Germany

I think I learnt quite a lot in Germany really. I learnt how to cooperate and and communicate properly with the Germans.

I learnt how to ask for things, and how to give the proper ammount of money that is asked for in a shop, for each item.

The best thing about the holiday is meeting people in the Youth hostel and making new friends. The worst was ~~there~~ the long journey. I believe it was the best holiday I had.

Assessing progress 8

In einer Waage gewogen und zu leicht befunden werden.

Assessment lies at the heart of learning and teaching a language and, like language itself, it is as simple or as complex as we choose to make it. *Sprechen Sie Deutsch?*

Simple - because we have a real-life model as a yardstick. Can you or can't you say it in German?

Complex - because as teachers we have to describe the stages in the language learning process of a number of individuals.

WHAT IS THE PURPOSE OF ASSESSMENT?

A national system of assessment involves attainment targets or objectives, and programmes of study which 'establish the matters, skills and processes which pupils should be taught in order to achieve the attainment targets'. How well the students are doing is monitored by **regular classroom assessment** carried out by teachers, by marking and recording and by external tests.

New systems are being devised to assess and report on all students under the National Curriculum, but Graded Objectives, GCSE and most of all Graded Assessment have already started to put many of the principles into practice (see Chapter 2). Whatever the new terminology, certain basic considerations still apply.

The **purpose** of assessment is to:
★ monitor progress;
★ report inside and outside school;
★ evaluate teaching;
★ support learning.

The **system** should:
★ be simple and practical for pupils, parents and employers;
★ involve pupils in self-assessment;
★ reward all aspects of achievement;
★ be credible, with efficient record-keeping and agreed marking policy;
★ be valid and reliable - should test what it claims to test and produce the same result whoever marks it.

WHAT DO YOU ASSESS?

What you know, understand and can do.
★ **Concepts and knowledge**
  e.g. vocabulary, how German works - grammar, *Landeskunde*.
★ **Skills**
  e.g. communicate by speaking or writing, transfer and adapt between contexts, understand what you hear or read.
★ **Attitudes**
  e.g. confidence, initiative, working cooperatively in class, pairs or groups, personal organisation and study skills

HOW DO YOU ASSESS?

- by continuous assessment. Listen to pupils practising role-plays in pairs. Record marks for speaking. Set tasks which involve finding out and then writing up.

- by regular tests involving all four skill areas, perhaps every half-term or 'unit'. These do not have to be formal tests in class. They could be homework or 'project' tasks.

- by agreeing short-term goals with the student and discussing whether these have been achieved.

- by setting some open-ended assignments in order to discover higher ability or extra talents.

Remember: if you integrate assessment into your normal teaching programme it will be less of a burden. Look for ways to accredit what pupils are doing in class without bringing progress to a halt while a formal test is carried out.

Less 'teaching from the front' is one implication of this.

MARKING

Just as any task set should have a purpose, so should your marking. Distinguish between correcting and marking. The point of correcting is that the student learns from doing the exercise and would do it better next time. Don't correct everything therefore, but focus on areas for improvement. Encourage re-drafting of work and ask students to assess it themselves. Mark mechanical or grammatical exercises for **accuracy,** but mark communicative tasks for **communication** and bear in mind other 'GCSE' criteria such as fluency, range and appropriateness of language, independence and accuracy. Make sure pupils understand what you are looking for and why. Try to agree a common policy in the department.

Why not simplify your marking by using the German system?

1. *Sehr gut*
2. *Gut*
3. *Befriedigend*
4. *Ausreichend*
5. *Mangelhaft*
6. *Ungenügend*

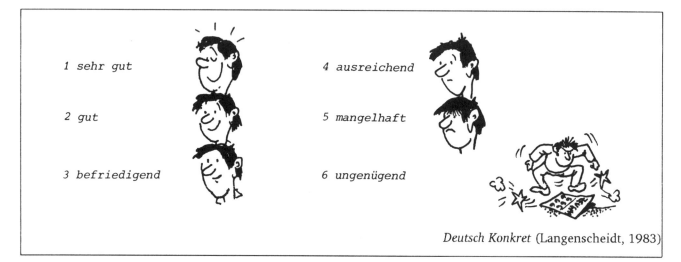

Deutsch Konkret (Langenscheidt, 1983)

SELF-ASSESSMENT

Ensure pupils understand the objectives of the course and the criteria used to measure their progress. By asking them to assess their own performance and by discussing what needs improving they will acquire a greater sense of responsibility for their own learning.

A progress card such as the one on the opposite page has tasks which the students tick when they think they are ready to be assessed. The teacher then awards one or two points.

FORMATIVE ASSESSMENT

Providing your 'tests' reflect your teaching objectives you should be able to diagnose the strengths and weaknesses of a student and set targets for improvement. This diagnosis should be clear in any report or profile.

SUMMATIVE ASSESSMENT

When students pass a Graded Test or complete a Level in a graded assessment scheme, they should receive a certificate or statement which describes briefly what they can do. This might be included in individual Records of Achievement.

PROFILING

Whatever local or national system operates, you will need to report on each individual's progress and describe what that individual can do. A profile should provide a brief course description (common to all students) and comments under headings such as ability to absorb and use new language, understanding of grammar and structures, listening, reading, speaking and writing skills, personal and social skills, motivation. There should also be a clear indication of progress towards tests, levels, GCSE.

In some profiling schemes, statements under these headings are kept in a computer 'bank'. However, even when writing out reports 'longhand' it is important to have in your mind a clear framework of areas for comment.

Remember: if you need to comment on pupil performance in a particular skill area:

- that skill area must be practised in the course;
- it must be assessed;
- the evidence must be recorded.

NATIONAL CURRICULUM

Under the National Curriculum there will be **prescribed** profile components and attainment targets, statements of attainment at various levels and **standard** assessment tasks, but these will be complemented by the teacher's own **continuous assessment**. In short, this means that it will be necessary to have differentiated descriptions of performance for pupils of all abilities. Graded assessment makes it possible to have students working on the same topics within the same class or age-group while their performance is assessed and recorded at different levels.

For a full departmental discussion of all aspects of assessment use the following in-service training manual from the NFER*: *Assessment in action: a guide for language teachers*

Above all, remember the golden rule for any system you devise: **keep it simple, valid and reliable**.

ENTERING STUDENTS FOR EXTERNAL EXAMINATIONS

When discussing with students which parts of the current GCSE examination they should be entered for - should they attempt Higher Level speaking or writing, will they have a chance of performing positively at Higher Level listening? - it is important to be able to base your discussions on evidence.

A record of regular assessments will complement mock examination results and may also indicate which type of course would be appropriate post-16 - 'AS', BTEC, FLAW, etc.

The point of a differentiated entry pattern for GCSE examinations is that it should allow students to maximise their scores in those areas in which they can do well. In the months leading up to the exam this allows them to concentrate their efforts on likely areas of success and not waste time. Putting candidates in for everything can be counter-productive.

PREPARING STUDENTS FOR EXAMINATIONS

Ensure that students are familiar with the format and style of the papers:

- are questions to be answered in English or German?
- are there choices or do you attempt it all?
- how should the time be allocated? How much detail is needed in an answer in order to gain full marks? Have all the questions asked in the stimulus letter or postcard been answered?

It remains unfortunately true at GCSE and at 'A'/'AS' level that **examination technique** is still a major factor in improving performance. Candidates should be trained to read the rubrics very carefully.

Ensure students are aware of the importance of giving their own opinions in an oral examination and that they should offer more than the minimum answer. They will need to listen and react to what the examiner says.

When preparing yourself to conduct the oral examination, consult the advice offered by the board very carefully and look for ways in which you can:

- develop a conversation naturally by moving from one subject to the next;
- use 'prompt' questions and suggestions rather than painstaking interrogation(!);
- give the candidate the opportunity to:
    - ★ cover the widest possible range of language;
    - ★ show command of a wide range of structures;
    - ★ offer individual reactions and opinions;
    - ★ take the initiative and show independence.

(See *Possible Model for General Conversation (GCSE)* opposite).

Do not underestimate the importance of vocabulary retention for success at even Basic Level. In fact, short items in Basic listening tests often amount to little more than an aural vocabulary test. Candidates whose gist understanding may be good in a real-life context with all its extra verbal and visual support may be defeated by the short disembodied utterance from the loudspeaker.

Expressions and phrases grouped in topic areas and logical situations will be memorised more easily. Some students might like to make a conscious effort to develop techniques for improving their memory and other study skills such as organising lists. Contact the Accelerated Learning Association, 50 Aylesbury Road, Aston Clinton, Bucks HP22 5AH or SEAL, Forge House, Limes Road, Kemble, Glos GL7 6AD. Send to CILT* for the subject guide: *Innovative methods in language teaching* (send 50p plus an A4 sae). Read *Superlearning und Suggestopädie* by R S Baur (Langenscheidt, 1990).

The GCSE word-lists issued originally by the examining groups for German have been much criticised. For example, a computer-assisted comparison showed that from a total range of 1800-2400 words on the word-lists for German only about 800 were common to all boards!

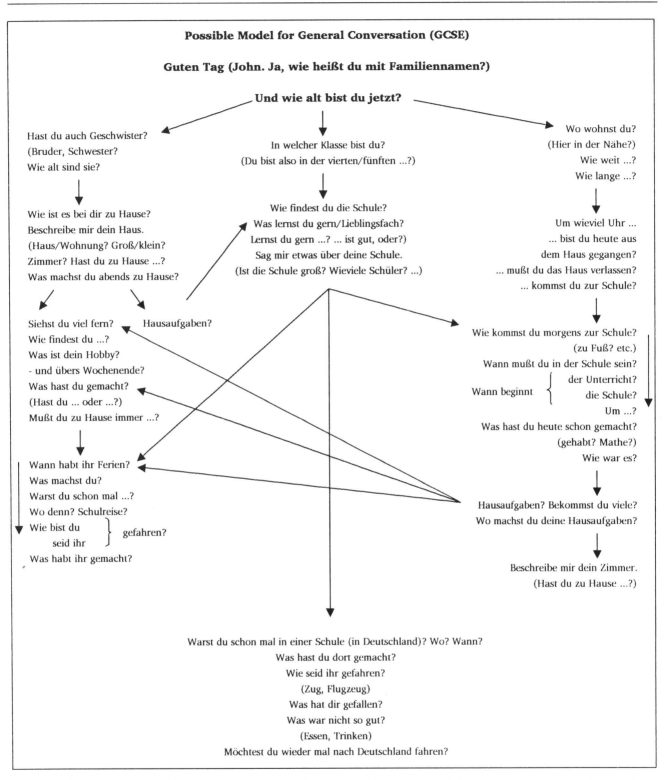

For a defined content syllabus supposedly based on real-life usage, such discrepancies are unacceptable and it is likely that word-lists will be replaced by a more flexible definition of areas of language.

Perhaps the most enjoyable way to increase lexical knowledge is to encourage more extensive reading (and listening). The APU survey into Foreign Language Performance in Schools (1983) showed that teachers underestimate the preparedness and ability of pupils to tackle **longer** texts. An emphasis on signs, notices and 'public' language would constrict pupils' exposure to longer and more interesting texts. A series of interesting booklets based on those findings is published by NFER/Nelson, Darville House, 2 Oxford Road East, Windsor SL4 1DF (Tel: 0753 858961 for prices).
Ask for the booklet on listening and reading.

THE SCHEME OF WORK

The foundation for success in examinations lies in a teaching plan which starts to prepare the pupils for the demands of the syllabus from the outset. Furthermore, under the National Curriculum students have an entitlement to a range of experiences and opportunities in their language lessons.

A scheme of work is a department's statement about current provision, aims and objectives and future plans. It has to be updated when necessary and all members of the department should be involved in its construction and review. It should not be set in stone but should constantly evolve and reflect what actually happens.

It needs to consider the following issues, all of which are addressed elsewhere in this book.

1. Aims - National Curriculum; GCSE National Criteria; school ethos/aims.

2. Objectives - National Curriculum attainment targets; exam syllabuses; differentiated objectives for all learners; cross-curricular opportunities.

3. Method - communicative approach; class organisation; learning processes and activities.

4. Assessment - what, how and when to assess; how to record information; marking policy; reporting and profiling.

5. Course structure - National Curriculum programmes of study; areas of experience, units, topics, roles and settings, notions, functions, grammar; skills; appropriate resources.

6. Resources - existing books, tapes, OHTs, videos; self-devised materials; hardware.

7. Staffing - structure, consultation and responsibilities within the languages department; in-service training and staff development.

8. Records/performance indicators - past test and examination results; record of journeys, visits and other activities; contacts with outside bodies, e.g. Goethe-Institut, local employers.

9. Destination of leavers, jobs using languages, FE or HE language courses.

10. Any evidence of customer satisfaction! - preferably via regular formal consultation.

Find out more by reading;

Assessment in action - a guide for language teachers. NFER (1989)

Peter Doyé *Typologie der Testaufgaben für den Unterricht Deutsch als Fremdsprache.* Langenscheidt (1988)

DES National Curriculum Working Group Report. (1990)

GCSE syllabuses and the GCSE National Criteria

Evaluation and testing in the learning and teaching of languages for communication. Council of Europe, Strasbourg (1988)

CILT Pathfinder Series:
Recording progress by John Thorogood. CILT (1990)
Schemes of work by Laurie Kershook. CILT (1990)

Taking it further 9

*Wem Gott will rechte Gunst erweisen,
Den schickt er in die weite Welt.*

Students need to have long-term goals as well as short-term objectives. At fourteen they should be aware of the training and vocational opportunities beyond sixteen and the progression routes of courses and qualifications, i.e. they should think 14-18 rather than 11-16. At sixteen they should be looking at Further Education and careers involving languages.

LANGUAGES AND CAREERS

Consult *Languages and careers - an information pack*, A King, Thomas, G and Hewett, D, CILT, new edition 1989.

This contains succinct but very complete information on Higher Education opportunities and especially on new language courses involving media, accountancy, business, science, etc. It also has information on examinations, booklets entitled *Working in languages* and *Your degree in modern languages - what next?*, information and resources lists for teachers, posters and a student's guide to working in Europe. This pack is an essential resource for any educational institution. You and your students can supplement it with displays of articles and advertisements about jobs involving languages.

There are also some useful videos available:

Why learn German? - Goethe-Institut/Inter Nationes (with leaflets, badges, etc for 11-15-year-old pupils).

Job talk: languages and the world of work
A 40-minute video with notes. Sections aimed at teachers, employers and students. The emphasis is on everyday situations involving foreign visitors in this country.

Details from: Focus in Education Limited, 365 Ewell Road, Tolworth, Surrey KT6 7DE.
Tel: 081 390 6768.

It is important to stress the value of a foreign language as an extra or secondary skill alongside a main qualification in another specialism. It is an asset in a wide range of jobs at many levels - from 16-year-old school leaver to university graduate. Discuss the career implications with students. Here is a list to start them off - how many more can they discover? (More ideas in the CILT pack).

Accountants, fashion designers, cabin crew, secretaries, librarians, tour operators, bank employees, lorry drivers, hotel receptionists, shop assistants, telecommunications, executives, lawyers, chefs, armed forces.

Languages and careers: an information pack by A King and G Thomas, with D Hewett (CILT, 1989)

CHOOSING THE RIGHT COURSE

For courses at universities, polytechnics and colleges of higher education ask your Head of Careers for the *UCCA handbook*, the *Polytechnic courses handbook* and the *Compendium of advanced courses in colleges of further and higher education.*

The CILT pack contains information on other publications which offer advice to assist students in making the right choice. See also *Foreign languages in industry and commerce* (Language Teaching Centre, University of York*).

CILT has produced (1990) *Degrees of fluency - the sixth former's guide to language degree* courses by Ann King. This contains extensive useful information on courses at universities and colleges, options, interviews, etc.

LINGUA

Look out for information from the **UK Lingua Unit***. This European Community action programme will be of interest to students planning a career involving languages at any level - whatever their particular specialism. Ask for the detailed Applicants' Guide which states precisely what grants are available for what purposes.

Under the existing ERASMUS programme of the EC, undergraduates are able to spend a recognised period of study in another community country and receive a grant. This is not confined to students of languages since a foreign language is valuable for **all** in Higher Education.

WILL STUDENTS NEED GENERAL SKILLS OR SPECIALISED SKILLS?

Even those who will later need German for business purposes are most likely to use it in the context of social and personal relationships. Companies are more interested in building on general language skills and cultural awareness than in specialised technical or commercial language. That sort of training is more effectively done as a short course later. One conclusion to be drawn from this is that GCSE represents a good foundation for likely future needs.

THE LANGUAGES LEAD BODY

Nevertheless, the Industry Lead Body, and the NCVQ (National Council for Vocational Qualifications) are currently working on definitions of national levels of language competency for vocational purposes against which all schemes or examinations will be measured. (Further information is available from The Languages Lead Body, CILT, Regent's College, Inner Circle, Regent's Park, London NW1 4NS. Tel 071-224 2296 Fax 071-224 3518)

Once employers have decided what their own needs are, they will be able to specify precisely, by reference to this national scale, what levels of competence are required for a particular job.

The implications for the providers of Further Education are profound, since potential students will have clear expectations of any course they undertake.

Professional development   10

*Wenn die Rose selbst sich schmückt,
Schmückt sie auch den Garten.*

As the demands on German teachers develop and expand in order to meet the requirements of a rapidly changing world, it is important to analyse your own personal needs both as a Germanist and as a teacher. Ultimately, we are all responsible for our own professional development.

LANGUAGE SKILLS

The Goethe-Institut* runs courses in Germany, usually in the Easter holidays. These are designed to improve teachers' own language skills and are particularly good for those seeking an intensive but enjoyable refresher course - especially where German is their second foreign language.

The Goethe-Institut offers, in fact, a wide range of courses and qualifications ranging from intensive residential courses in all parts of Germany to longer term courses involving weekly classes at the Institut here. Contact your 'local' Goethe-Institut* for the relevant brochures.

Another way of improving your linguistic skills is by arranging a teacher exchange for anything from three weeks to a year with a colleague in Germany. Contact the Central Bureau* for information on their teacher exchange, study visit and short course programmes.

The Lingua* programme (see previous chapter) will also promote in-service training of teachers and exchanges of teachers.

METHODOLOGY

CILT provides a programme of national and regional conferences and in-service training 'to order' for institutions or local authorities. An annual list of courses is published jointly by CILT and the Central Bureau. Your institution should receive a copy. It is available direct from CILT. CILT has also a comprehensive information and resource section as well as a long list of its own publications designed to meet teachers' needs. Send to CILT for: information sheets on *The CILT language teaching library* and *Research in focus - sources of information on research in language teaching,* and the *CILT publications catalogue.*

The Goethe-Institut* organises a programme of one-day conferences, evening meetings and workshops dealing with aspects of German teaching.

The Language Teaching Centre at the University of York* offers annual courses for teachers of sixth forms and also a one-year full-time course or a two-year part-time course leading to an Advanced Diploma in language teaching.

The Mary Glasgow Language Trust (c/o CILT*) offers a fellowship each year. This provides for three months' secondment on full salary to a British university in order to pursue a project on language teaching/learning.

The Association for Language Learning (the unified association for everyone concerned with teaching and learning foreign languages) holds a three-day conference every spring with workshops, talks, presentations and displays on all aspects of languages. Information via ALL*. There is also a German in-service day.

German Teaching is the journal of the German Committee of ALL and appears twice yearly. It is an invaluable collection of articles, reviews and information on courses and anything and everything of interest to German teachers.
To join ALL contact The Secretary General, Association for Language Learning, 16 Regent Place, Rugby CV21 2PN (0788 546443).

Your local education authority may have its own programme of in-service training related to national priorities such as assessment and records of achievement. Specialist provision for languages varies enormously from one LEA to another. Contact your local teachers' centre, advisory teacher, adviser or inspector - ask what opportunities exist for professional development and suggest what you would like to see.

SCHOOL-BASED IN-SERVICE TRAINING

Your school should have a development plan with identified whole-school priorities. Look at cross-curricular issues such as equal opportunities, personal and social education, special educational needs and information technology. Clarify in your own mind what contribution your subject can make to a broad and balanced education for each student. Recognise areas of weakness, learn from other subject areas and, where possible, from other schools.

FUNDING

Under a system of Local Management of Schools, with in-service funding devolved to individual institutions, it is even more important that you make a well-argued case. Emphasise the attractions of German for potential 'customers' and also the particular contribution and relevance of German to the individual, to the community and ultimately to the country as a whole. As a German teacher you are a valuable and relatively scarce asset. Claim all the support you require.

As Goethe said:

Nur die Lumpen sind bescheiden,
Brave freuen sich der Tat.

Bilden wohl kann der Verstand, doch der tote kann nicht beseelen,
Aus dem Lebendigen quillt alles Lebendige nur.

Useful addresses

Associated Examining Board (AEB)
Stag Hill House
Guildford
Surrey GU2 5XJ
Tel: 0483 506506

Association for Language Learning (ALL)
16 Regent Place
Rugby CV21 2PN
Tel: 0788 546443

Association for Modern German Studies,
Bruce Watson, Department of German
Royal Holloway and Bedford New College
Egham Hill
Egham
Surrey TW20 0EX
Tel: 0784 34455

Austrian Embassy
18 Belgrave Mews West
London SW1X
Tel: 071 235 3731

Austrian Institute
28 Rutland Gate
London SW7
Tel: 071 584 8653

BBC Education
Villiers House
The Broadway
London W5 2PA
Tel: 081 743 8000

BBC English
Sales Office
P.O. Box 76
Bush House
London WC2B 4PH
Tel: 071 257 2886/2851

BBC Publications
32 Marylebone High Street
London W1M 4AA

Books in German
Romy Freiburghaus
6 Barnfield
Blackstone Edge Old Road
Littleborough
Lancs OL15 0JL
Tel: 0706 72252

Brighton Polytechnic
The Language Centre
Falmer
Brighton BN1 9PH
Tel: 0273 606622

Business and Technician Education Council
(BTEC)
Central House
Upper Woburn Place
London WC1H 0HH
Tel: 071 388 3288

Central Bureau for Educational Visits and
Exchanges
Seymour Mews House
Seymour Mews
London W1H 9PE
Tel: 071 486 5101

3 Bruntsfield Crescent
Edinburgh EH10 4HD
Tel: 031 447 8024

16 Malone Road
Belfast BT9 5BN
Tel: 0232 664418

52 GERMAN

Centre for Information on Language Teaching
and Research (CILT)
Regent's College
Inner Circle
Regent's Park
London NW1 4NS
Tel: 071 486 8221

City and Guilds of London Institute
76 Portland Place
London W1N 4AA
Tel: 071 580 3050

The Copyright Licensing Agency Limited (CLA)
33/34 Alfred Place
London WC1E 7DP
Tel: 071 436 5931

DER Travel Service
Deutsches Reisebüro
16-17 Orchard Street
London W1H 0AY
Tel: 071 486 4593/7

Deutscher Volkshochschulverband (DVV)
Prüfungszentrale
Eschersheimer Landstr. 61/63
D 6000 Frankfurt 1

The European Bookshop Limited
4 Regent Place
London W1R 6BH
Tel: 071 734 5259

German Embassy
23 Belgrave Square
London SW1X 8PZ
Tel: 071 235 5033

German Student Travel Service
Terminal House
52 Grosvenor Gardens
Lower Belgrave Street
London SW1
Tel: 071 730 2101/3227/3225

German Tourist Facilities
184 Kensington Church Street
London W8 4DP
Tel: 071 229 2474

Goethe-Institut
50 Princes Gate, (Exhibition Road)
London SW7 2PH
Tel: 071 581 3344

Ridgefield House
14 John Dalton Street
Manchester M2 6HG
Tel: 061 834 4635

The King's Manor
York Y01 2EP
Tel: 0904 611 122

3 Park Circus
Glasgow G3 6AX
Tel: 041 332 2555

Goethe-Institut Head Office
Goethe-Institut, Zentralverwaltung
Postfach 20 10 09
D-8000 München 2

Hatfield Polytechnic
German Centre
College Lane
Hatfield
Herts AL10 9AB

Inner London Educational Computing Centre
(ILECC)
John Ruskin Street
London SE5 0PQ

Institute of European Education (IEE)
St Martin's College
Bowerham
Lancaster LA1 3JD
Tel: 0524 32423

The Institute of Linguists
24a Highbury Grove
London N5 2EA
Tel: 081 345 0202

Inter Nationes
Kennedy-Allee 91-103
D5300 Bonn 2

International Baccalaureate
c/o University of London
Institute of Education
18 Woburn Square
London WC1H 0NS
Tel: 071 637 1682

International Baccalaureate
Office du Baccalauréat International
Route des Morillons 15
CH-1218 Grand-Saconnex
Geneva
Switzerland

Joint Matriculation Board (JMB)
Manchester M15 6EU
Tel: 061 953 1180

Lingua Unit (UK)
Seymour Mews House
Seymour Mews
London W1H 9PE
Tel: 071 224 1477

The London Chamber of Commerce and Industry
Examinations Board
Marlowe House
Station Road
Sidcup
Kent DA15 7BJ
Tel: 081 302 0261

London and East Anglian Group (LEAG)
EAEB, The Lindens
Lexden Road
Colchester
Essex CO3 3RL
Tel: 0206 549595

London and East Anglian Group Graded
Assessment Section
Stewart House
32 Russell Square
London WC1B 5DN
Tel: 071 436 5351 ext. 4707

Midlands Examining Group
UCLES
1 Hills Road
Cambridge CB1 2EU
Tel: 0223 61111

National Centre for CALL (NCCALL)
Ealing College
1 The Grove
London W5 5DX
Tel: 081 579 4111

National Council for Educational Technology
(NCET)
Science Park
Coventry CV4 7EZ
Tel: 0203 416994

National Foundation for Educational Research
(NFER)
The Mere
Upton Park
Slough
Berks SL1 2DQ
Tel: 0753 74123

Northern Examining Association
Joint Matriculation Board
Manchester M15 6EU
Tel: 061 953 1180

Northern Ireland Schools Examining Council
Beechill House
42 Beechill Road
Belfast BT8 4RS
Tel: 0232 704666

Oxford and Cambridge Schools Examination
Board
Elsfield Way
Oxford OX2 8EP
Tel: 0865 54421

The Royal Society of Arts Examination Board
John Adam Street
Adelphi
London WC2N 6EZ
Tel: 071 930 5115

School Journey Association
48 Cavendish Road
London SW12

Scottish Consultative Council on the Curriculum
17 St John Street
Edinburgh EH8 8DG
Tel: 031 557 4888

Scottish Examination Board
Ironmills Road
Dalkeith
Midlothian EH22
Tel: 031 663 6601

Scottish Vocational Education Council
Hanover House
24 Douglas Street
Glasgow G2 7NQ
Tel: 041 248 7900

Southern Examining Group
AEB
Stag Hill House
Guildford
Surrey GU2 5XJ

Swiss Embassy
16-18 Montague Place
London W1H 2BQ
Tel: 071 723 0701

University of London Schools Examination Board
(ULSEB)
Stewart House
32 Russell Square
London WC1B 5DN
Tel: 071 436 5351

University of Oxford Delegacy of Local
Examinations
Ewert Place
Banbury Road
Oxford OX2 7BZ
Tel: 0865 54291

University of York
Language Materials Development Unit
The King's Manor
Exhibition Square
York YO1 2EP
Tel: 0904 27844

University of York
Language Teaching Centre
Heslington
York YO1 5DD
Tel: 0904 433954

VISCOM Limited
Unit B11
Park Hall Road Trading Estate
London SE21 8EL

Welsh Joint Education Committee
245 Western Avenue
Cardiff CF5 2YX
Tel: 0222 561231

Notes

STANLEY THORNES
 Cheltenham 0242-228888